SURVIVING M&A

SURVIVING M&A

Make the Most of Your Company Being Acquired

SCOTT MOELLER

A John Wiley & Sons, Ltd., Publication

This edition first published 2009
© 2009 John Wiley & Sons, Ltd

Registered office
John Wiley & Sons Ltd, The Atrium, Southern Gate, Chichester, West Sussex, PO19 8SQ,
United Kingdom

For details of our global editorial offices, for customer services and for information about
how to apply for permission to reuse the copyright material in this book please see our
website at www.wiley.com.

Wiley also publishes its books in a variety of electronic formats. Some content that appears
in print may not be available in electronic books.

Designations used by companies to distinguish their products are often claimed as
trademarks. All brand names and product names used in this book are trade names, service
marks, trademarks or registered trademarks of their respective owners. The publisher is not
associated with any product or vendor mentioned in this book. This publication is designed
to provide accurate and authoritative information in regard to the subject matter covered.
It is sold on the understanding that the publisher is not engaged in rendering professional
services. If professional advice or other expert assistance is required, the services of a
competent professional should be sought.

Library of Congress Cataloging-in-Publication Data

Moeller, Scott.
 Surviving M&A : make the most of your company being acquired / Scott Moeller.
   p.   cm.
 Includes bibliographical references and index.
 ISBN 978-0-470-77938-5
 1. Consolidation and merger of corporations.   2. Corporations–Employees.
I. Title.   II. Title: Surviving M and A.   III. Title: Surviving mergers and acquisitions.
 HD2746.5.M644 2009
 650.14–dc22

                                                                    2009022483

Set in 11.5/15pt Bembo by SNP Best-set Typesetter Ltd., Hong Kong
Printed in Great Britain by TJ International Ltd, Padstow, Cornwall, UK

This book is dedicated to my four children:
Christine, Andrew, Ellen, and Jonathan.
They amaze and inspire me every day.

CONTENTS

LIST OF FIGURES

LIST OF SPOTLIGHTS
(CASE STUDIES)

FOREWORD

Next time, it won't be me

"I bet you all have heard it before: The 'merger of equals' announcements, the 'we will keep the best talent' slogans, and the 'possible layoffs will be announced as soon as possible' promises.

The first time I went through a merger, I simply assumed everything would be sorted out for me, that I definitely belonged to the 'best talent', and that I was safe if they didn't tell me in the first four weeks to leave. When they told me 12 weeks into the merger that my role had become redundant, I couldn't believe this was happening to me. They told me it had nothing to do with me, but it was the role. I was shocked, I was not at all prepared, and I took it personally.

Certainly, it helped to see other colleagues facing the same fate. However, I couldn't stop thinking that, at the end of the day, 10% of all staff of the combined company had lost their jobs. Why was I one of them, why did I not belong to the other 90%?

Five years into a job with another company, we learned that we had bought our biggest rival. Excitement mixed with anxiety as memories of the past bubbled up. Surely, I needn't feel frightened? I was a senior manager, I was employed by the company which took over the other, and surely this time I would get involved in any decision making about future org charts?

I did get involved. Over the following eight weeks, I was working with my team day and night on strategy papers for the combined firm, on the client story, the key messages for our client-facing staff, and I had no time whatsoever even for a second to wonder whether I was doing enough and if there was anything I could do to not face the same situation again. I felt safe, I felt being an important part already of the enlarged firm. Wasn't all the work I've been doing the best proof that my role was now even more needed? Didn't my boss tell me every so often during these weeks how happy he was with my team's output?

I did feel safe, yet I was fired on the day they announced record half-year earnings for the combined company, six months after the announcement of the acquisition had been published. It hurt like hell. I felt humiliated, stupid, a loser, but mainly I felt like a fool.

Three weeks ago, we were told a US firm has bought us. I'm thoroughly enjoying my job here and occasionally think that I wouldn't be where I am now, happier and quite success-ful, without those two − at the time − bad experiences. Still, this time I don't want to wait to see what fate has in it for me. This time, I'm managing my own destiny. This time, I won't allow myself to be a victim. Plan A naturally is to keep my job. I think there are a few things I can do to help with that. But even if it doesn't work out and I might hear 'you're fired' for a third time, I'll be equally prepared.

If I get told to leave, then Plan B is to depart with my head held high."

Senior manager, sales and marketing, financial services

CHAPTER 1

HOW TO USE THIS BOOK

Mergers and acquisitions have a life of their own. No one, not even the chief executive officer (CEO) of the company, can control the changes taking place once an acquisition or merger is announced. Employees often feel like pawns in a chess game, but so do senior managers. Yet in the midst of all this chaos and turmoil, it is possible to bring more control to your future if not even improve your position with the new company.

Two companies merge. Or a big company takes over a smaller one. Sometimes it's two competitors, or maybe it's a company buying just one division of another. A hedge fund or private equity firm acquires a start-up or failing firm. Possibly even three similarly sized companies come together to create a new organization. No matter what the form of the merger and acquisition (M&A) deal, what's one of the first things to happen? An announcement by the new management that there will be a round of layoffs. Employees are fired. Whole teams are made redundant.

In different companies and countries it's called different things: jobs cuts, layoffs, redundancies. But they all mean the same thing: people are losing their jobs. The official announcement will typically say that somewhere around 5–15% of the total workforce of the two companies will be made redundant.

> **The painful truth about most mergers**
>
> "It's inevitable. If we acquire a company, we'll make people redundant."
>
> *Michel Akkermans, Chairman and CEO, Clear2Pay*

A survey conducted in 2002 by consultants Towers Perrin found that 46% of companies going through mergers and acquisitions made immediate job cuts; further layoffs followed because of the deals, often several years later. In the USA, over 150 000 redundancies annually are due to organizational changes including mergers and acquisitions, according to the Bureau of Labor Statistics in 2008. These numbers are huge. During times of recession (and, in some industries, depression) such as the economic downturn that started in 2007, the number is likely to be even higher as yet more firms merge or get acquired as they run into financial difficulties.

Emotions run high when there's news – even just a rumor – of a pending M&A deal. Such news can be "toxic" to a work environment which was once attractive to employees who had been committed to the company and engaged by their work. That previous employee engagement is replaced with selfish concerns about individual job security and other personal objectives such as which position they will assume in the new organization. From the company's perspective, it becomes very difficult to retain employees or attract new employees until the deal is completed and, often many years later, settled. Even in more benign mergers, where the promise of the deal is high, staff fear that there's a hidden management agenda to cut headcount or to use the acquisition to claw back attractive employment conditions. It's no wonder that employees are concerned. *The New York Times* reported in 1998 that over 75% of laid-off women do not have another job after one year. Other studies claim that nearly 75% of all Western households have a family member or neighbor who has been laid off.

Most employers do have the best intentions in mind: they want to treat all employees fairly, but are also under pressure to show cost savings through layoffs. Managers try to be fair, focusing on a "correct" selection process (frequently asking outside consultants to advise and assist) and providing compensation above the statutory minimum in combination with counseling and outplacement support. Others, however, don't realize the side-effects of conducting redundancy badly. They communicate poorly, comply only with the minimum law requirements, and stretch the process out over time, making the experience even more stressful for redundant employees. They cause an even greater amount of stress, fear, and even resentment not just in the people being told to leave, but also for those who remain.

Anything seems better than living through the hell of a merger or acquisition …

"I'm going to wash beer mugs in a biker bar – better pay, better hours, and a better class of people!"

A banker following redundancy, as quoted in Here is the City, *a London-based news and careers website*

Everyone reacts differently to the news of an M&A deal affecting their company, and they react differently again when they are told how it might or will affect them personally. Why do some people do better in a deal than others? Does it depend on whether you work in the front office or back office? Are some types of people able to exploit the situation more effectively? Is it purely a political game? Or is it just luck?

Many books have been written about how companies can be more effective at merging – focused on the organization, longer-term strategic positioning, cultural integration, and the financial results of the proposed M&A deal. As it is important to the companies in structuring a deal, those books will also make a distinction between a merger (usually when the two organizations are of similar size and when they together create a new third company so both prior companies cease to exist) and an acquisition (when one company, typically the larger one, acquires the second company and then the second company ceases to exist and becomes part of the first). Those distinctions are not critical in this book – as no matter how structured, people are fired in most deals. Accordingly, most of the comments in this book relate to either situation.

Instead of a focus on the companies merging or acquiring, this book focuses on the personal situation of employees who are experiencing an M&A deal right now or who have recently been told that their company will be acquiring, taken over, or merged. It is intended for use by individuals as a guide to how to exploit for personal benefit a situation of corporate change which, in this case, is caused by a pending M&A deal. As many corporate or private equity (also including venture capitalist and other financial) buyers have discovered, one of the greatest challenges within the M&A process involves people-based decisions – who to retain and who to keep.

A common wedding joke applies to mergers as well

A wise person once said that a beautiful marriage is one in which two people become one. The trouble starts when they try to decide which one.

The personal impact is significant. Following redundancy, employees suffer both financially and socially (including lack of self-esteem and standing among friends and colleagues). This book will hopefully provide people facing this situation with a practical guide to various situations and illustrate scenarios with "sound-bites" from people who have had personal direct experience in being survivors or victims of mergers and acquisitions.

The reason for layoffs is often the result of a very rational strategic process within the company making the acquisition. From a financial perspective, the reason for many mergers is to improve the company's competitive advantages and to benefit from economies of scale. One way to achieve the necessary and promised cost savings from a merger is via downsizing the workforce: firing people who thought they had secure jobs. Some people made redundant – usually in senior management – will receive attractive severance payments and retain some of their corporate benefits including medical and life insurance or share bonuses.

Even for those who gain some benefits and definitely for those who find themselves with no work at all, it will be a traumatic experience. While many employees may prefer to drag out the redundancy process and stay with the company for as long as possible in order to maintain their current pay and benefits until they find a new job, others prefer to be put out of their misery and go quickly as they feel that the waiting and not knowing is even worse. The Chartered Institute for Personnel and Development (CIPD) found in its 2008 annual survey of absence management that organizational change and restructuring, including acquisitions and mergers, can be the largest cause of work-related stress in some organizations.

There are thousands of M&A deals annually, even in years when the level of M&A activity is "slow." These deals are often front-page news and, especially when there are many layoffs as part of the deal, they receive intense media focus. Mergers and acquisitions therefore have become an inescapable part of most people's lives – directly or indirectly. Few employees anywhere will have a career in which they don't face a situation when their company merges, acquires, or is acquired – or faces the possibility of one of those. How you react will affect the outcome for you.

This book focuses on layoffs due to mergers and acquisitions, but the larger number of employees facing redundancy for other reasons may also find helpful tips in this book. Although up to one-third of a company's workforce may involuntarily or voluntarily leave because of a merger or acquisition, most redundancies do not take place because of M&A but rather for general business reasons such as a decline in sales, changes in technology leading to discontinued products and services, outsourcing, and other factors. Research at Cranfield Business School on executive redundancy and outplacement in 1993 in the UK showed that only 7% of redundancies were due to restructuring following a merger or takeover, yet, almost a decade later, in 2002, a CIPD redundancy practices survey found that this figure had almost doubled to approximately 12%. Since the UK Office for National Statistics places the number of redundancies in recent years at around a half million employees annually, this means that over 60 000 people have their employment terminated each year in the UK because of mergers or acquisitions. Thus, together with the figure of M&A redundancies in the USA mentioned earlier, these two countries alone have up to 200 000 people fired annually because of M&A deals. Again, the number is likely to have grown significantly when taking into account the more recent impact of M&A deals during the economic downturn that started in 2007.

This book isn't really designed for employees whose future with the company is dependent on the negotiating talent of others. Thus, if you are a member of a trade union or represented by a works council or other multi-employee bargaining representatives (or their equivalent, as these differ by country), then although the first part of this book might provide some useful background to situations you find yourself in, it is unlikely that you will be able to employ many of the suggestions that have been made by those interviewed. Unionized workers were not interviewed; union negotiations during mergers are beyond the scope of this book.

This book does not look at factors where it would be illegal in most countries to discriminate in favor of or against a group of employees or any individual, such as sex, race, country of origin, age, sexual orientation, physical or mental disability, or religion. I can say that in the research conducted for this book, no such widespread discrimination was uncovered, but it was also not the focus of the research and the interviews and surveys did not ask about it.

Most of the interviews for this book have taken place in Europe and the USA, although many of those conversations have been with individuals who have worked in multiple locations around the world or who had started their careers elsewhere: from throughout Asia, South America, Russia and the former Soviet republics, Australia, and Africa. Research has been conducted to ascertain whether the comments made are generally applicable to other non-US or Western European cultures. In many cases they are not, but then many of the comments are company specific or even specific to a particular group or situation within one organization.

Although cultures differ, the general recommendations from this book are applicable globally. For example, in a study of a merger between two Chinese internet companies conducted at Cass Business School, target employees were found to have much lower job satisfaction after the deals were completed than the acquirers, which is consistent with "Western" deals. Remarkable consistency does exist where I have looked at different countries and cultures. Where there are differences, these will be noted.

HOW THE INFORMATION FOR THE BOOK WAS COMPILED

Prior to the publication of this book, the extremely broad M&A landscape has been evaluated predominantly from the corporate and human resource management perspectives with many of the books and much of the research focusing on how deals deliver shareholder value through increased market share and better financial management, including use of resources (such as employees, but treating them mainly as costs to the firm and not as people). Little had been written from the perspective of the employee, and this book is hopefully a start in that direction. Even books with similar titles about "surviving M&A" have focused more on how the company can survive without providing advice on what individual employees should do.

Naturally, as discussed later, it is critical that the company survives, because most deals fail and no one has a job with a company that no longer exists. Assuming that the company will survive, this book will address how you can, too.

Most of the people interviewed for this book, who have lived through mergers and acquisitions, were managers or employees of the companies that combined, and almost equally distributed from the target or buyer. Others were advisors: human resource consultants, investment bankers, strategy and public relations consultants, funding banks, venture capitalist and private equity firms, lawyers, journalists, and academics. Literature in the area was not extensive, but has also been reviewed (with a number of useful articles and books shown at the end of this book). The result is hopefully a useful list of suggestions that provide a new focus on individual benefit rather than that of the company. And if enough individuals feel better as survivors, this may also contribute to the future success of the deals from the company's and shareholders' perspective as well. One can hope.

This book is based on my professional experience of more than 30 years working in investment banking and mergers and acquisitions, beginning in the mid-1970s as a strategy consultant (at Booz Allen & Hamilton, now Booz & Co., in Washington, DC, New York, and London) helping companies planning acquisitions and then almost 20 years in two investment banks at

Morgan Stanley and Deutsche Bank (being based first in New York, then Tokyo, Frankfurt, and lastly London). In both of those firms, I was responsible at different times for acquisitions being made by those companies, and in founding and running a venture capital group that made a large number of acquisitions as well (in total, having principal responsibility for well over 30 acquisitions and assisting with numerous others). Following that, I began teaching Mergers and Acquisitions in graduate business schools, first at Oxford University, then Imperial College London, and, since 2002, at Cass Business School in London where I also founded and am the director of the M&A Research Centre. While teaching, I continued to advise companies on their mergers and acquisitions, and have written (often together with my students) a number of published case studies, including the acquisition of Manchester United Football Club, Abbey National Bank (by Banco Santander), and the recent merger of The Bank of New York and Mellon Financial. The research for this book began when writing *Intelligent Mergers: Navigating the Mergers and Acquisitions Minefield*, which was co-authored with Professor Chris Brady and published in 2007.

In writing this book, I have complemented my own first-hand experience in the industry with formal and informal interviews conducted during the past two years with over 100 people who have been through M&A deals from all organizational levels, many countries, and virtually every industry. In the course of several projects as part of their dissertations, supervised students in the academic year 2007/8 have conducted further in-depth interviews or surveys of over 250 individuals who have lived through a merger or acquisition (although a global group, most of these interviewees or survey respondents were from the UK and other parts of Western Europe, due to the location of Cass Business School in London). See also the acknowledgements for further information about these surveys. Many people have therefore kindly shared their survival tips with us: these have included suggestions about actions that they took which they felt were successful in making them a survivor of an M&A deal, or that they observed others doing well. There were also many who told us they were not successful in retaining a position after their company was acquired; these individuals described what they wished they had done differently or suggested things that they did which they shouldn't have. The stories they told, as well as some of their direct quotes, are included throughout the book.

Most hadn't consciously developed a grand plan for how they succeeded. Luck was mentioned often as a key factor … and it is. In a number of interviews, people either quoted Robert Burns ("The best laid plans of mice and men/go oft awry") or another quotation often attributed to Napoleon ("I would prefer a lucky general to a smart one"). Another senior manager interviewed put it even more simply: "The Number One factor is luck." Combined, these stories provide powerful ideas for those currently facing possible redundancy because of an M&A deal – and possibly facing redundancy for any reason.

The role of luck in being a survivor

"I got the job because there was nobody else. The acquirer's senior manager retired during the deal."

Head of legal, European bank

Most of these interviews took place around the time when the economy and the M&A markets were beginning to decline (2007) or when they were even in freefall (in the second half of 2008). The banking and economic crises therefore did provide a backdrop to many of the discussions, causing a number of interviewees to comment that their suggestions were particularly relevant to redundancies in general, and not just when firms merge or acquire. Certainly, although the volume of M&A deals did decline in that period as discussed later, they did not disappear.

The need for survival in a company that was merging was perhaps even more important because fewer other firms were hiring.

ALL LEVELS OF ORGANIZATION

Focus turns inward. When a company is in turmoil because of merger or acquisition, people begin to think about their own future and that is when personal issues become paramount. Company business becomes less important to many – at the exact time when proving your value to the company is perhaps most important. People cannot, and perhaps should not, avoid this internal focus. Interviewees often said that it was critical to "look out for Number One," as quoted above. Others noted that the word "merger" starts with "me."

No matter in which company you sit (acquirer or target), news of a merger or acquisition will cause a roller-coaster of emotions with more "lows" initially than "highs." It won't matter whether you're a senior executive and maybe had even been one of the architects of the deal, or a temporary worker who had been with the company for only a short time. Front office, middle office, back office – all are affected (although sales staff usually find that they can protect themselves most easily, as discussed later).

A lot happens once you find out that your company is being acquired. Information is usually scarce and accurate information is even more difficult to find. Loyalties are divided: do you rely on those you have been working with, or do you try to align yourself with the new company? Your confidence is lower because of the uncertainty. And it's not just you. There's a general feeling of insecurity throughout the company that is easy to sense and very infectious.

Productivity therefore declines as everyone tries to find out what's really happening. People start to take action – sometimes any action! – to position themselves best. The politics becomes both more unclear yet more intense as power structures shift and people begin trying to figure out who's in and who's out. These concerns and issues are often strongest among middle managers who used to think that they had some control but now appear to have none – they are too low in the organization to be "insiders" to the deal, yet are seen by their teams as people who should know what's going on. The fact is that all employees often feel the exact same stresses and uncertainties, although at different times.

Just as bidding company employees tend to be improperly complacent, senior executives very often also have their heads in the sand regarding the likelihood of their staying with the company after the deal closes. They are very much at risk. A 2003 study in the *Harvard Business Review* noted that, for the nine years following a merger, executive attrition averaged 20% per year for companies that had merged, whereas it was only 10% annually for non-merged companies. Other studies show executive turnover around 50% following a purchase. Many of these executive departures will have been voluntary resignations, but even these are often made only after the managers realized that they didn't feel comfortable working in the new organization because of the changes that the merger or acquisition caused. At the time when the deal was announced, and even soon thereafter, they may have had no intention of leaving ... but the deal can cause those feelings to change over time.

DESIGNED FOR ALL PHASES OF THE DEAL

Companies don't need two of everything: certainly not two CEOs, two sales people covering the same client, or two heads of human resources. But being the one made redundant isn't always bad. When a company goes through a merger or acquisition, it may be the perfect time to make a career change. M&A situations may be a welcome catalyst for many to leave. These deals can bring new opportunities and open new career paths for some, but for most forced to leave the company, it is an unwelcome if not devastating change.

A lot of people consider that an M&A deal ends when the transaction closes, with the two companies becoming one. But that's not correct because at this point the focus of the deal merely shifts internally and the most daunting and time-consuming process of combining the two companies starts. This is called "post-merger integration." Integration plays a more significant part in the success of the deal than any other step in the M&A process and certainly lasts much longer (often years) than the deal completion process itself, which is usually over within a few months.

It is, of course, best if you read this book *before* a deal is announced, or when there are only just rumors of a pending deal. That time, or even immediately after you hear officially that a deal is taking place, is when most employees will still refuse to accept that it will take place. It is unfortunately unlikely that many will pick up this book then. It's more likely you're reading this book days or even weeks after you first heard that your company was being taken over or was being merged with another. The deal may not be over, but at least now looks unstoppable.

But even if the deal has already closed and the new company formed, there are tips and suggestions that will still apply to that long post-deal closing period. In most mergers and acquisitions, it takes time before they settle down, and maybe even years, as noted above. It usually isn't clear to senior management at the time of the announcement who should stay and who should leave. In fact, those managers may have designed a post-merger integration process specifically intended to determine who will be asked to leave and also to remain. This book provides a number of useful suggestions for improving your odds of being selected to stay.

ACQUIRER OR TARGET?

Some people think that if it is their firm acquiring the other company, they are safe. After all, it is their managers and their company in control. Most of the time they are also much bigger than the target company. But the thought that you are safe is dangerous and may lead to complacency. Why? Because at the same time as you are *not* doing anything to secure your job, the target company's employees – who naturally think they are more at risk (and they are!) – will be fighting hard for any job, including yours. So, in many instances, they do take advantage of the complacency of others and land the job. The acquirer's employees may never know what hit them.

From the target company's side, it is usually obvious that their employees are more likely to be laid off than employees from the larger acquirer. When the Royal Bank of Scotland acquired the investment banking division of ABN AMRO in 2008, the *Financial News* reported only 27% of the overlapping senior positions went to the target's managers from ABN AMRO. Therefore, as target company managers and employees expect to land fewer of the positions after the acquisition, it is likely that from the start that they will be thinking carefully about whether they want to leave or stay and, if they decide to fight to stay, how they will do it.

In a merger (where two essentially equal companies come together so there isn't either an acquirer or a target), it will be a mix of the above. There may be even more confusion in the organization because it is less clear who will be on top and which culture will be dominant, whether a different culture will evolve that is a mix of parts of both organizations, or even something totally new.

PUBLIC AND PRIVATE

The need for cost efficiencies when two organizations merge – and thus the resulting need for layoffs – doesn't discriminate between public, private, or non-profit firms. All face the same pressure to reduce headcount when two organizations are put together. In conducting interviews for this book, a large number were in public and non-profit organizations, and their stories and suggestions varied little from those in the private sector.

Differences do exist, however. Deals tend to take place faster in the private sector, although this is not always true. Public sector organizations seem to use different criteria for making people redundant. According to the CIPD redundancy practices survey mentioned earlier in this chapter, public organizations tend to select employees for redundancy based on performance and/or efficiency, whereas the private sector uses individuals' roles or positions within the organization. The survey noted that employees made redundant in the private sector can potentially feel more stress as they either feel they had yet to show their full potential or, in the case of executives, they worried that their management techniques had been discredited.

TOP TIPS

A useful summary of many of the suggestions and comments about surviving M&A is included in the "Top Tips" (see Figure 1.1). These ideas will be developed further in this book as many overlap and some even appear inconsistent with others as every merger situation is different. Look over the list at this point to get an idea about what others may have found useful or wish they had done differently when faced with the need to survive an M&A deal. All the survey respondents had experience with at least one merger or acquisition, and some with several. Most mentioned a number of tips, as usually it is best to take several actions even simultaneously, as will be discussed later. While reading the list, keep the following in mind:

Rank	Recommended actions to survive a merger
1	Find ways to add value
2	Be proactive
3	Maintain a businesslike attitude
4	Position yourself so your skills will enhance the new organization
5	Become invaluable to the acquiring company
6	Impress the decision-makers at your company
7	Keep a positive attitude
8	Embrace what is happening
9	Look at the merger as a challenge and an opportunity for growth
10	View challenges as opportunities
11	Be patient – don't make rash decisions about your role
12	Be helpful (both to senior and junior colleagues)
13	Be a problem solver for the new company
14	Promote your capabilities
15	Understand the new partner's objectives
16	Determine the culture and your role in the merged entity – can you be comfortable there?
17	Ask questions
18	Assess carefully whether you want to stay
19	Expect change, don't resist it
20	Take the opportunity to demonstrate your worth
21	Get as much information as you can about the deal
22	Participate in planning sessions
23	Come to terms with what is happening and move forward
24	Portray your skills and accomplishments in the best light
25	Volunteer to serve on a transition team
26	Establish which company is the dominant player
27	Be visible and make direct contact with your new colleagues
28	Identify a function you perform well and make sure everyone knows it
29	Assess the political situation
30	Maintain a sense of humor about the situation
31	Brace yourself for a change
32	Research the new company and its management
33	Be easy to manage
34	Don't rely on your boss – in a merger everyone looks out for themselves
35	Treat the merger/acquisition process like an extended interview
36	Try to understand the reasons behind the changes
37	Don't be a complainer
38	Identify with your profession and not your company
39	Utilize your network, both social and professional
40	Update your skill sets
41	Prepare a contingency plan
42	Stay in constant touch with colleagues in other organizations doing similar work
43	Adapt to the dominant culture
44	Manage personal stress
45	Spend more time in the office to develop relationships
46	Update your *curriculum vitæ* or résumé and look for a new job
47	Maintain the status quo
48	Keep your head down
49	Transfer loyalties to new management as soon as the deal is announced
50	Enlist the help of a business/career coach

Figure 1.1 Top 50 tips

Source: Dickenson and Wood, Cass Business School (2008)

- Each company and each acquisition will be different and therefore some actions may not apply.
- Acquisitions and mergers evolve: any action should be adapted for appropriateness at different stages of the deal.
- Don't rely too much on any one action, as noted above; it is possible to combine these suggestions. The use of one tip may actually support success with other tips.
- Be realistic as some actions may take too long, require assistance that isn't available, or may not fit your personality.
- Don't continue to put effort into a strategy that isn't working; be willing to try different actions when one isn't working, but be patient as well and don't discard an action prematurely.

The book will further discuss how to use the tips and suggestions later, including how these individual actions can link to each other, thus enabling you to have a plan for survival.

ORGANIZATION OF THE BOOK

As not all the suggestions will be relevant for everyone in every situation, it is recommended that each reader make a careful assessment about which ideas will be helpful to their own personal circumstances and the work culture of their existing or future employer. Also, some people will already have experienced a merger or acquisition before, whereas for others it is their first time. Therefore, Part I of the book provides a description of the M&A landscape: what these deals are from the company's perspective, how companies combine, why they do it, and who the professionals are behind these transactions. It also explains why these deals affect employees, how people feel, and why certain individuals might do better when their companies merge, acquire, or are acquired. Part II of the book then provides the suggestions for bettering your chances of surviving the merger, starting with a discussion of whether you really should try to stay or not. Those very familiar with M&A deals can probably skip directly to the second part to find these ideas that should help them survive.

PART I

WHAT HAPPENS?

CHAPTER 2

WHY SHOULD I BE INTERESTED IN M&A?

I f your company's not in the middle of a merger or acquisition, should you care about whether you would be a survivor if it were? Many survivors of deals said that they wished they had laid the groundwork before any deal had been announced, as by the time the announcement was made, it was too late for many. Finding out that your company is being sold is always a surprise, except to the very small handful of people inside the company who have planned the deal. In some takeovers, even the CEO and board are caught unawares that they are a target. At the time a deal is announced internally to employees, there are usually more external advisors who know about it – but are sworn to secrecy – than there are internal employees and managers who know. The book will discuss these advisors later.

Many of these mergers and acquisitions veterans of at least one deal said that they would have been at an advantage over other employees if they'd taken some of the steps noted in the book before they even dreamt a deal would take place. They also felt that some of the tips and suggestions would help them in terms of being "business savvy" about how to be best positioned in a company even if the company isn't merging with another. Those same veterans suggested that it's more likely than not today to experience a major M&A deal at some point in your working life – and many times during a career if you're lucky (or perhaps unlucky!).

EVERYONE'S AFFECTED AT SOME TIME

Many employees feel that their company is safe. They feel that their company is too successful to be a target, or that it is too big to be bought, or that their company doesn't need to acquire another company because everything is working fine: revenue growth, profitability, satisfied customers, and happy employees.

This may have been true 30 or 40 years ago (and maybe not even then), but certainly is not so today. Deals are common where the purchase price is in the billions of dollars. In the five-year period from 2004 to 2008 (including the recent financial crisis of 2007/8, which witnessed a number of mega deals to save some of the world's largest banks and financial institutions), there were over 300 announced takeovers or mergers worth over $5 billion. If companies this large are at risk, then almost any company is. Note the case below on the acquisition of Gillette by Procter & Gamble (P&G): Gillette was over 100 years old and very success-ful, yet it still became a target. This deal will be used again to illustrate several points, as one of my students was able to speak to a number of employees from both firms about their merger experiences.

Spotlight: Procter & Gamble/Gillette

Employees unprepared

In January 2005, Gillette was acquired by P&G for $57 billion at an 18% premium for the Gillette shareholders. The combined company had about $60 billion in revenues. Twenty-one brands had revenues of over $1 billion. It became the largest company in its industry, overtaking the previous leader, Unilever, in both market capitalization and revenue. The merger resulted in around 6000 job cuts which was equal to 4% of the combined workforce of the two companies.

P&G itself was established as a result of a merger in 1837 in Cincinnati by William Procter and James Gamble when they combined their small businesses to produce and sell candles and soap. By 2004, P&G manufactured and marketed over 300 branded products which were sold in more than 160 countries.

Gillette had a proud and long history as well, having been set up in 1901 by King Gillette and William Nickerson. In 1904, they patented the double-edged safety razor, which became the shaving standard for decades. Gillette quickly expanded into foreign markets and by 2004 was operating in more than 200 countries.

But the process of post-merger integration of these two companies faced resistance. In one country where one of my students interviewed a number of people who were with Gillette at the time of the acquisition, we were told that they had joined what they thought was a long-term employer with sufficient size and famous brands. They felt that Gillette was a leader in the industry on many fronts, including their internal operations. For example, on the technical side they saw a gap of five to seven years between the information technology (IT) infrastructure of Gillette and P&G. "We had to move from modern IT systems to Excel tables," noted one Gillette employee after the acquisition.

Not only were some Gillette staff personally unprepared for the takeover, because they often felt that their company was the better one, they also didn't believe in the "tremendous opportunities" that were promised by top management from P&G. Gillette employees had to face the unpleasant dilemma of either moving to P&G (and coming to terms with the changes) or leaving the company.

P&G and Gillette essentially had two different corporate cultures, we were told. Employees of Gillette hoped that Gillette, because they had been so large and successful, would be able to influence P&G post-acquisition. But hoping for that "was a complete utopia," as one former employee said. Gillette was absorbed into P&G and very little from its culture was left, another said. Rather than change, employees voluntarily but reluctantly left the jobs they thought they would have until retirement.

But it is important to mention that not all employees were affected in the same way by the acquisition. Some were lucky – employees who worked in such business segments as Braun (electric razors) and Duracell (batteries) weren't affected much because P&G had no similar businesses and these divisions therefore largely continued to operate as they had prior to the acquisition.

For most employees, once they've heard that a deal is under way it will be too late to take many of the actions that would help them survive. It is therefore critical to anticipate deals and understand why they occur and when they are most likely to happen.

INTRODUCTION TO MERGERS AND ACQUISITIONS

Acquisitions and mergers are now so commonplace that they sometimes don't even make the front page anymore. It is now an accepted and even integral part of the strategy of large and small firms alike to restructure through the process of either acquiring or merging with other companies in whole or in part. In some industries – such as technology and pharmaceuticals – being acquired soon after start-up is even a sign of success for the founders, who may then move on to develop another company that they hope to sell to a larger competitor as soon as they can. Such serial entrepreneurs make a career out of being acquired.

Thousands of deals take place annually. Most are small and don't make the headlines. Yet even in small deals people are affected – you, if you work there, maybe a neighbor, or your father or daughter. People are working for each of those companies, and they have mortgages or rent to pay and families to support. They worry when they hear the news and don't know whether they will have a job when the two companies combine.

Merger and acquisition activity goes in waves (see Figure 2.1). There are years when there are record volumes of deals, and then a few years later the size of the market will be a fraction of the peak. Even in the troughs, the activity levels since the mid-1990s have been huge, and have exceeded the peak years of the 1980s. Thus, M&A activity in absolute terms never truly goes away and remains robust every year. There may be years when it is less

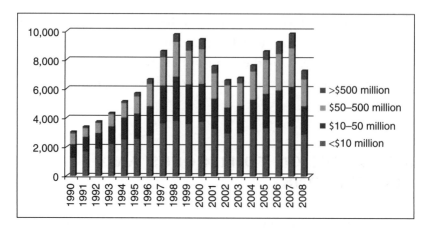

Figure 2.1 Number of completed deals grouped by size of the acquisition

Source: Thomson Financial (2009)

likely that deals will take place, but the threat of acquisition never goes away.

In late 2008, for example, when the overall global economy was reeling from the financial crises and over-leverage of the previous few years, and the entire world was entering recession, there were almost as many M&A deals canceled as announced. Yet the volume of completed deals in that "down" year was higher than the average for the 1990s, which itself had been a record decade for M&A. No longer are M&A deals special: the timing of any one particular deal may surprise the market (and these will be as big a surprise to most of the employees at the two affected companies as well), but the fact that such deals are taking place isn't a surprise anymore.

As can also be seen Figure 2.1, although there is great volatility in the number of deals, globally since 2000 over 6000 companies annually have been purchased, even in the "slow" years. Most of the deals are for companies that are considered to be very small (although the acquirer may in fact be much, much bigger). Consistently, over one-third and often almost half the deals done each year are for the purchase of companies that are bought for less than $10 million, but these represent less than 1% of the value of the deals done in any year. Conversely, the largest deals – those over $500 million – typically represent just under 10% of the number of deals but over 75% of the value. These are the deals that have the huge numbers of job losses, as discussed in the next section. Since there is such a large human element to the acquisition or merger, it's not surprising that it is these mega deals that get talked about on the 10 o'clock news.

It isn't clear what percentage of companies every year are involved in a merger or acquisition because figures on the total number of companies worldwide vary widely, but the mere number of deals as shown above is huge. It is why many of the people interviewed for this book said that one piece of advice is to always be prepared that your company will be acquired. Given the actual number of deals taking place, that is good advice.

HOW MANY PEOPLE ARE MADE REDUNDANT?

On average, approximately 10%–15% of a company's headcount will involuntarily or voluntarily leave during or following a merger. Not all of these job cuts are immediate but can take place many years later, although by that time the decision for an employee to depart may include other reasons as well, and not be exclusively due to the takeover having taken place.

When they combine, companies plan to cut anywhere up to 30% of the merged entities' workforce (see Figure 2.2). This is usually within the first year or so following the closing of the deal. Although many times the company will offer voluntary redundancy or achieve some of the reduction in workforce through natural attrition, most of the job losses are involuntary. Later,

Bidder name (or larger company if merger)	Target name	Business description	Date	Estimated job losses	% of total workforce
Daimler Benz	Chrysler	Automotive/Industrials	1998	26 000	20%
Bank of America	Merrill Lynch	Banking	2008	24 000	8%
Royal Bank of Scotland/Fortis/Santander	ABN AMRO	Banking	2007	19 000	9%
Hewlett Packard	Compaq	Information technology	2002	17 900	12%
Glaxo Welcome	Smithkline Beecham	Pharmaceuticals	2000	15 000	14%
Bank of America	Fleet	Finance	2004	13 000	7%
SBC	AT&T	Telecommunications	2005	13 000	6%
JP Morgan	Bear Stearns	Banking	2008	12 000	7%
JP Morgan	Bank One	Banking	2004	10 000	7%
AT&T	Bell South	Telecommunications	2006	10 000	3%
Alcatel	Lucent	Telecommunications	2006	9 000	10%
Exxon	Mobil	Integrated oil	1999	9 000	7%
Nokia	Siemens (carrier)	Telecommunications	2007	7 500	13%
Verizon	MCI	Telecommunications	2005	7 000	3%
Procter & Gamble	Gillette	Personal care	2005	6 000	4%
Telewest	NTL	Telecommunications	2006	6 000	31%
Bayer	Schering	Pharmaceuticals	2006	6 000	10%
British Petroleum	Amoco	Integrated oil	1998	6 000	6%
Deutsche Bank	Bankers Trust	Banking	1999	5 500	6%
CGU	Norwich Union	Insurance	2000	5 000	7%
Oracle	Peoplesoft	Information technology	2004	5 000	9%
Santander	Abbey	Banking	2004	4 100	3%
Chevron	Texaco	Integrated oil	2000	4 000	7%
Bank of America	Lasalle	Finance	2007	2 500	3%
The Bank of New York	Mellon	Finance	2007	3 900	10%
Commonwealth Bank	Colonial Bank	Banking	2000	2 900	7%
Thomas Cook	My Travel	Travel/Holiday	2007	2 800	15%
Worldcom	MCI	Telecommunications	1998	2 300	3%
Boots Pharmaceutical	Alliance Unichem	Pharmacy/Healthcare	2006	2 250	2%
AA	Saga	Insurance	2007	2 000	18%
Orange	Wanadoo	Telecommunications/Internet	2006	2 000	15%
Grand Metropolitan	Guinness	Beverages	1997	2 000	9%
Delta Airlines	Northwest Airlines	Airline operators	2008	2 000	3%
Nationwide	Portman	Banking	2007	1 800	8%
Ericsson	Marconi	Telecommunications	2005	1 200	15%
TUI	First Choice	Travel/Holidays	2007	1 000	6%
Carrefour	Promodes	Supermarket	1999	0	0%

Figure 2.2 Redundancies announced for selected mergers and acquisitions

Source: Company announcements and press reports

during the stabilization stage of the deal, other employees may decide independently to leave because of continuing organizational instability, uncertainty, and a change in the corporate culture or management that they don't like. Once these departures are taken into account, the figures of "turnover" often exceed the target percentages and reach levels that are unsettling to the company. "Regretted departures" (as they are called in many companies) include people the company really wanted and needed to keep, but the fallout of the deal has caused them to leave.

What do merger and acquisition mean?

The terms "merger" and "acquisition" tend to be used interchangeably under the broad term "M&A" as, in most cases, it is a subjective view on what form of deal is actually occurring. Strictly speaking, as noted in the first chapter, an acquisition is when one company takes over another company which is usually smaller; the target then ceases to exist. Typically, when characterized as a "takeover" there are hostile elements to the deal as the target company is actively resisting being acquired. For public companies, this means that the board of directors opposes the purchase and recommends to their shareholders not to approve the deal. On the other hand, "mergers" are almost always friendly and usually take place between two companies of similar size in the same industry. In a merger, both companies cease to exist and a new company is formed from the combination. In this book, where the distinction between a "merger" and an "acquisition" is important in terms of how an employee should act, this will be noted; most of the time, however, the precise formal structure of the transaction is not crucial and the terms will be used interchangeably.

Popular usage, including in the business press, mixes up these terms because it often isn't clear what the ultimate outcome will be. There are also instances when management have decided to characterize the deal as either a "merger" or "acquisition" for internal or external political or cultural reasons. For example, communications teams and senior management in many acquirers will call their acquisition of a smaller company a "merger" because it then gives the appearance of being friendlier with a sense of equal opportunity for staff from both firms. They may want to emphasize as well that they really are serious about seeking the best from both firms with the goal of creating a new and better firm. Or they may want the employees of the target to feel they are empowered in the new organization, as otherwise the typical first reaction of the staff of any target is to feel a loss of control and a lack of "being wanted" by their new employer, as will be discussed later in this book.

No matter whether the deal is officially structured as a merger or an acquisition, the final culture and leadership of the newly combined companies can often take years to settle. At all levels, there will be winners and losers: one company's culture and managers will come out on top and many employees will be made redundant.

Why deals happen (and headcount cuts are often the reason)

No matter how characterized, the vast majority of M&A deals are opportunistic and political even if the public announcement is full of business justifications for the deal. The decision to merge or acquire is therefore as much emotional as rational, and usually has aspects of both. For any single individual in the company, their survival will depend on how they can position themselves to benefit from the deal, even if the reasons for the deal may be unclear and decisions about retaining employees political and subjective.

A typical press release announcing the deal with great fanfare will typically mention several very compelling justifications for the merger or acquisition being in the best interest of both companies; these press releases will imply or even explicitly refer to a long-term strategic and financial planning process that resulted in the decision to proceed with the particular deal. In reality, these reasons for the deal may have been developed *after* the deal had first been discussed and perhaps even after the initial negotiations took place. The justification for the deal may have been developed afterwards to assist in persuading employees, shareholders, suppliers, clients, regulators, and others that the deal makes business sense and to gain the support of those key stakeholders in the two firms.

Those stated reasons for M&A deals fall under three broad headings: strategic, financial, and organizational. These are not mutually exclusive. Any one deal may incorporate more than one reason for the deal taking place. No matter what the reason for the deal, layoffs are likely to occur, and this book will highlight where there are important differences in the approach to redundancy depending on the underlying reason for the deal.

- **Strategic:** where the plan is to increase market share, improve products or systems, focus the business, or reduce competition. These are acquisitions or mergers where the two companies are in the same or related business areas, and the intent is to strengthen the combined companies' market position. Such strategic acquisitions can be vertical, where a company acquires a supplier or distributor further up or down the production chain and sales process. Alternatively, they could also be horizontal, which would put two competitors together with cost savings from workforce reduction, elimination of duplicated functions, and economies of scale in manufacturing, distribution, marketing, and virtually any other area of the business.

Example of a strategic deal

"We were the larger company, based in Belgium, acquiring a similar French company. We were two technology companies: our product had functionalities that their product didn't. Although we were the acquirer, their product would be the surviving one, but could be improved with some of our product's functions. We needed to integrate their know-how and experience. We wanted their customers, too."

Michel Akkermans, Chairman and CEO, Clear2Pay

Any strategic move can stimulate changes in the industry if the deal is the first of its kind and large enough, or could be made as a defensive response to a competitor's deal if another group of companies had initiated their own merger first. It is often beneficial to be the first in an industry to do such a strategic merger or acquisition: a company can therefore make sure that it – and not another firm – will benefit from the advantages of being combined with the target company.

Acquisition to get there first

"There was no way we could have let our competitor buy them. If we had done that then we'd be dead in the water ... Could you imagine?"

CEO, financial services firm

Figure 2.3, from a survey of US CEOs, illustrates the frequency of certain strategic and commercial reasons for conducting M&A deals. Note that the reasons add up to much more than 100% because in most deals there are multiple reasons given for the deal taking place.

According to 44% of CEOs in the same survey, strategic M&A deals differ from financial deals because in strategic deals

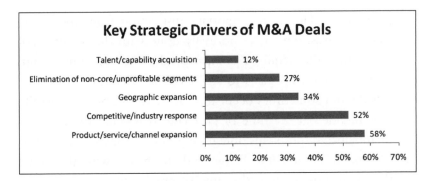

Figure 2.3   Key drivers of M&A deals
Source: Towers Perrin, *HR Rises to the Challenge: Unlocking the Value of M&A* (2004), reproduced with permission

there are opportunities to extract synergies. As will be shown later, these synergies normally translate into a tremendous number of job losses. There will also be significant job losses if the strategic deal is redefining the industry, as whole areas of the company may become redundant if no longer needed.

- **Financial:** where the money involved principally led the deal. These deals are predominantly opportunistic and usually occur because a company can be purchased at a "bargain" price. In periods of economic downturn, such as in 2008 and 2009, there may be many undervalued companies that get purchased by rich financial buyers such as sovereign wealth funds from the Middle East and Asia; some of these purchases would not have taken place when the economy (including those companies) was stronger and their price higher.

  Financial acquisitions can be made by any company or even an individual investor, but are most commonly made by private equity firms, venture capitalists, or hedge funds. As such, they are not acquisitions for the long term, as these buyers ultimately plan to sell the acquired company when they can make a profit – selling the company for more than they paid for it. This is an important distinction from the above strategic deals, which are normally done with the intention of integrating the acquired company fully into the buyer and, therefore, with no plans to sell it off in the future. (Not that this doesn't sometimes occur in strategic deals, but was usually not intended at the time of purchase. It is often the result of unanticipated problems integrating the company once it is bought or because the buyer finds problems with the target that were unknown at the time of purchase.)

Financial deals cannot usually extract the kinds of synergies that exist in strategic deals, but that doesn't mean that there aren't redundancies following the acquisition of companies for financial reasons. Many, if not most, of the deals done principally for financial reasons are highly leveraged deals, as the increase in debt on the part of the buyer provides the opportunity to increase the acquirer's profit when the acquisition is ultimately sold. This leverage brings much higher fixed costs in terms of paying the monthly, quarterly or annual interest on the debt, which in turn leads to a very strong immediate need for financial buyers to reduce the expenses of any company they purchase. This includes making people redundant. Most studies have found that the level of job losses in financial deals is larger and faster than in strategic deals.

Not all financial deals are done to make a profit on the later sale of the company. They can also be strategically financial, for example to take advantage of tax losses in a target company (which can then be used by the acquirer) or to buy a business that can improve the purchaser's capital structure (lowering borrowing costs or using surplus cash from the target). Although it is usually less critical for the buyer to lay off employees quickly in these deals, there are still some redundancies made.

- **Organizational:** where the purchase of a company is dominated by the personal ambition or "hubris" of senior management, typically the CEO. Although rarely stated publicly, the personal desire of managers driven by ego has been a principal driver to deals since the first merger wave of the 20th century when individuals such as John Rockefeller, Andrew Mellon, and J.P. Morgan put together their oil, steel, and banking empires. Governments now step in to prohibit deals that would produce too much market concentration, but within the restrictions of anti-trust and monopoly laws and regulations, CEOs still believe that "big is better and even bigger is even better." Many observers would attribute hubris to a number of takeover bids in recent years, such as Sir Philip Green's unsuccessful attempt to purchase Marks & Spencer in 2004, the 2007 acquisition of ABN AMRO by a consortium of banks led by Sir Fred Goodwin's Royal Bank of Scotland, and the 2008 purchase of Merrill Lynch by Ken Lewis's Bank of America. In all these deals, there were huge numbers of job losses projected when the deals were announced; in the deals that did complete, some of the first to be made redundant were the overlapping senior managers.

Ego driving the deal

"I didn't want to end my career quietly ... I wanted to be remembered as a household name in the industry."

CEO, retail firm

There are deals done for other organizational reasons as well. Some of these may not have large numbers of redundancies. These include mergers and acquisitions to get people (key managers, sales people, and other talented and experienced employees) and diversify from the core business by buying into unrelated businesses (although since the 1960s the stock markets have punished companies that are conglomerates and a whole industry of restructuring firms make their money from finding such companies and breaking them up in what are largely financial deals).

As can be seen from the above discussion of the three principal drivers to M&A deals, no matter what the actual or stated reasons given, virtually all result in situations where people need to be made redundant, whether because of the need to eliminate overlapping jobs or because of the necessity to reduce costs. A personal "employment defensive strategy" is therefore needed for anyone in a company where such a deal may be likely or already under way.

Most fail – so you can win the battle but lose the war

Most deals fail, no matter what drove the companies to the point of combining. Study after study has confirmed this, no matter what criteria have been used to determine success (whether seeing if shareholder returns have been improved, the acquired companies are retained or sold off later, the announced goals of the acquisition have been achieved, growth has been accelerated, etc.). These studies, including a number conducted at Cass Business School on a global basis, show that only 30–40% of most mergers and acquisitions are successful. It is therefore very likely that an individual employee can win the battle (remain an employee and not be made redundant because of the deal) but lose the war (ultimately being laid off anyway because the company eventually fails because of the deal).

Mergers fail

"Most mergers fail. If that's not a bona fide fact, plenty of smart people think it is. McKinsey & Company says it's true. Harvard, too. Booz Allen & Hamilton, KPMG, A.T. Kearney – the list goes on. If a deal enriches an acquirer's shareholders, the statistics say, it is probably an accident."

The New York Times, *February 28, 2008*

While some failures can be explained by market factors, a substantial number can be traced to neglected human resources issues and activities. Historically, plenty of attention has been paid to the legal, financial, and operational elements of mergers and acquisitions but the people side has often received little focus. Executives are now recognizing that in today's economy, the management of the human side of change is the real key to maximizing the value of the deal. Thus, the focus on surviving and assisting the survivors becomes a virtuous circle that makes the success of the deal from the company's perspective even more likely, too.

Spotlight: Carrefour/Promodes

The CEO kept his job immediately after the deal but was later forced out

"In 2000, the agreement between Carrefour and Promodes [two French retail companies] was announced as a merger of equals. Both sides soon learned to dismiss such talk as politically correct but inaccurate, given the differences in company culture. If Carrefour was from Mars, then Promodes could have come from Venus. Carrefour maintained a Darwinian system of natural selection, while Promodes' working style could be described as collegiate. Within the merged company, leadership struggles grew ever more fierce, a number of Promodes' top managers quit the group, and the survivors clearly understood that Carrefour had gained the upper hand. Yet such control proved illusory, as the leading shareholder turned out to be none other than the former owner of Promodes. By 2004, Carrefour's CEO was forced out and top management was restructured along hybrid lines combining leaders from both companies."

Ory Eshel, Director of International Development, Carrefour

The M&A process

M&A deals are complex and can take years to complete. They are often the most difficult change in a company's lifecycle. There are a number of stages in an M&A deal and experts have described the process as having up to 16 steps. From the perspective of planning your survival, it is most helpful to think about four major stages, as shown in Figure 2.4.

HOW TIMING AFFECTS EMPLOYEES

The time from the start of the first phase through to the beginning of the fourth stage can vary greatly in length, from three or four months (and, in rare cases, even less) to several years. When a large organization takes over a much smaller one, the process typically is at the shorter end of this range (unless the acquirer intends to keep the target separate, in which case most employees are not affected because there is no real integration). Mergers of equals or acquisitions between two very large organizations tend to take the longest amount of time and may not enter the stabilization stage until two, five, or even 10 years after the deal announcement.

Spotlight: Procter & Gamble/Gillette

Timing and activities in the Procter & Gamble acquisition of Gillette

After Procter & Gamble acquired Gillette in 2005, at least in some countries two integration managers were appointed from each side. They negotiated the future structure of their organization, decided who to appoint to the new positions, etc.

In one division, a group of employees from Gillette were appointed to "close" Gillette during the six months prior to the actual close of the deal. In those six months, they managed effectively to freeze a company which was running at full speed. Then, in order to integrate people in departments, a grade scale was drawn for both companies. It was used to find out which positions in Gillette matched the corresponding level of positions in P&G. After that, a plan for the new organization was made and it was determined how many people were required to fill in any new positions. There were meetings of top management every week where key problems were discussed.

Ultimately, it took P&G about two years to implement the full integration process in that division.

Stage 1, the period leading up to the announcement, can take months (typically from three to six months), although during this time as noted in Figure 2.4, there is usually only a very small group of insiders in the firms who are aware of the deal and these typically would be at very senior levels or within a planning or corporate development team only.

The duration of Stage 2 is shown in Figure 2.5 which is from a 2007 study by DLA Piper, a global law firm. It shows that between one-half and three-quarters of deals completed this stage in less than six months, but note that some took even more than a year, especially corporate (principally strategically-driven) deals. Notably, the deals by financial buyers (such as private equity firms, venture capitalists, and hedge funds) were much faster with almost one-quarter completed in less than three months and only 3% taking longer than a year.

Stage	Description
Stage 1: **Pre-announcement**	• Senior management and outside advisors planning the pending merger or acquisition. Some discussion of the level of redundancies necessary when the deal completes. • Limited contact between the two companies, if any; the target company may not even know it could be acquired. • No public disclosure of the pending deal, but information leaks and market speculation can cause rumors and even premature announcement. • Internally, both organizations are still unchanged because most employees are blissfully unaware of the pending announcement. **Implication for employees:** Few employees are taking any action to enhance their survival post-announcement.
Stage 2: **Pre-closing**	• The period between the official announcement and the formal closing of the deal when the two companies become one. • Initial decisions on senior management changes and organizational structure are made. Best practice would have the first level of management determined by the time the deal is announced; each additional layer of management should be announced every six or eight weeks, but this often doesn't happen until later. • Joint committees or teams are formed to develop detailed implementation plans for the next stage, and the companies conduct due diligence on each other, including staff. Names of employees to be made redundant start to be compiled. **Implication for employees:** Most employees begin jockeying for positions in the new organization, but this is difficult because the final structure is still in flux. Rarely are employees laid off during this stage, but some will be told that they or their departments will be redundant. Competitors will begin poaching employees early in this stage and some managers and staff will decide to leave before waiting to hear if they will have a job in the new organization.
Stage 3: **Operational** **combination**	• This is when the actual post-merger integration of functions and operations takes place. Some departments will be combined quickly, some will not be affected at all (if they have no overlaps with the other company), and some changes will be planned to take many years to complete. Certain divisions may be sold if they are not needed in the new company. • Interaction between the two companies extends throughout the organization at all levels. **Implication for employees:** Employees try to adapt to the new organization. Some leave voluntarily. Others are made redundant, perhaps in multiple waves. Competitor poaching of employees continues. Many employees are still waiting to decide if they want to stay with the company long term.
Stage 4: **Stabilization**	• Changes and adjustments continue, but gradually diminish and are more due now to external changes in the marketplace and less because of the acquisition or merger. • The new culture and organizational structure are accepted by the remaining employees as "business as usual." There are fewer and fewer references to the way things were done in each of the prior companies. "We" culture has developed; it's no longer "us and them." **Implication for employees:** The remaining employees are those who intend to stick with the organization long term. These are the survivors. No further rounds of redundancies occur as a result of the combination of the two companies.

Figure 2.4 Four stages of an M&A deal

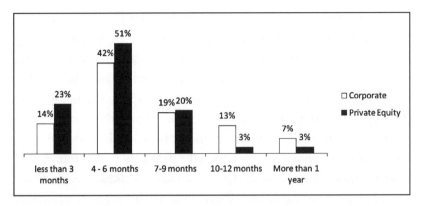

Figure 2.5 Timescale for an acquisition

Source: DLA Piper, *European M&A Survey 2007*, reproduced with permission

Spotlight: Burroughs and Sperry

Integration taking "forever"

"I joined Unisys back in the mid-1980s to run the Software and Services Division across Europe and Africa; circa $200 million business. Anyway, as part of my job I did a lot of manage-by-walking-about across the 14 countries that reported into me. The first question I was always asked: 'Where are you from?' This seemed strange at first as I was from the Unisys European Head Office and they all worked for Unisys in each country, but the real question was 'Are you from Burroughs or Sperry?', the two companies that had merged weeks before I joined and had formed to make Unisys. It took about five years for the question to be stopped being asked, as they still disliked each other and acted as if they were still in competition."

Steve Robson, founder, EA Consulting

Another factor that can cause a deal to take longer to complete is when the deal is hostile. Management of the target will be trying to defend the company from the unwanted takeover, delaying the process as long as possible both to deter the bidder and also to build its defenses. As will be discussed later in Chapter 5, employees in the target company after a hostile deal are more likely to be made redundant than if the deal was friendly. Because these do typically take longer to complete than friendly deals, they also represent a longer period of uncertainty for the acquirer's employees as well.

The last two stages are when there is the greatest variability in timing. The most intense period for the company as a whole (and now representing both companies that merged) is the first three months after closing. This period is sometimes communicated to the employees as "The First 100 Days" and is usually full of special communications and events to mark the combination of the two firms and the launch of the newly combined businesses. Although in many cases the frenetic activity may stop at the end of those first 100 days, as noted above, some very complex mergers aren't complete until years after the deal closing. For example the Morgan Stanley/Dean Witter merger (which will be discussed later) took over a decade before the last vestiges of the old companies were finally eliminated. These long integrations cause additional stress for management, clients, and certainly for employees who may be trying to decide throughout whether they fit the new culture and wish to stay with the company.

Long mergers cause human resource problems

"The acquisition was two years ago and we are not fully integrated yet. Our internal employee satisfaction rates are still low which shows that the company is tired. We now experience lower staff retention rates."

Head of strategy and consultancy, public health and
social work organization

M&A deals for most employees are therefore more akin to a marathon than a sprint. An early win may be ephemeral if the deal keeps on changing – as most do – through a long closing period and an even longer integration phase. One manager in a manufacturing firm told us that there were massive differences between the "Day 1" organization chart and what it turned out to be a year into the combination. He went on to say that if he'd relied on the position he thought he had secured soon after the deal was announced, then he would have been out of a job because it was eliminated. He said he needed to keep his ear to the ground throughout the merger process. Others, as in the case study below, found that the deal didn't turn out well for them for a couple of years.

Two years to figure out the merger wasn't for him

"I was close to upper management when the merger was announced and therefore easily slotted into a more senior position. I quickly learned that I didn't really know much about the position and neither did my manager. I spent the better part of two years spinning my wheels as I watched my peers get involuntarily and voluntarily separated. I tried to keep up with the needs of the business that seemed to change almost daily.

"After two years of valiant effort, I had the chance to take a voluntary separation package, and took it. Why? My mind wasn't being worked anymore. I was frustrated with the lack of leadership and poor morale. I wasn't being challenged anymore. Work wasn't fun. The small company feel that I loved was taken over by a bigger corporate image. I had to close my company's stores almost every week and was on the team of people who had to communicate that the workers of these stores would not have a job anymore. The emotion of the experience changed from one of great opportunity and a new/higher position to one of pain and thanklessness. I had to hear friends of mine who were good customers complain that the service was now very poor and that they were going to switch to another firm because it was just too expensive now."

Head of sales, professional services firm

IMPACT ON ORGANIZATIONS

An acquisition which initially appears to be a disaster from the corporate perspective might in fact turn out to be a success and do well financially provided that the post-merger integration is handled properly. The inverse is even more true: an acquisition that is based on sound strategy may in fact become a disaster if significant attention is not paid to the post-integration process. From the perspective of the employee, being able to anticipate which situation will occur is critical to the decision whether to put the effort into being a survivor ("winning the battle") because you certainly don't want to invest your valuable time and effort in a company destined to go bust ("losing the war" referred to earlier).

Long deal and integration process, ultimate failure

"The whole process was massive, lengthy, testing, and failed ultimately for lack of clarity and culture."

Head of department, manufacturing firm

KEEP AN EYE ON TOP MANAGEMENT AND OTHER CHANGES BEING MADE

How do you anticipate what's going to happen? Realize first that mergers and acquisitions are clearly one of the most extreme and complex forms of transformation that any company can experience. There will be conflicting signals. Some will point clearly towards success but most will be ambiguous, at least in the first stages of the deal. It is important to look clearly down the organizational change path because it is closely linked to change at the employee level. Organizations only change if the managers and employees also change, and senior executives usually lead that process.

Following on from that observation, research conducted in 2008 by Cass Business School graduate student Anita Longman provides what is perhaps the best indicator of success that each employee should be tracking once a deal is under way: the selection of the top team. In a survey which she conducted, the selection of the top team was ranked by 95% of survey respondents as either the "most" or "somewhat critical" people issue, closely followed by retention of key staff by 93% of respondents. If the new company is not demonstrating agreement about who will run the company at the top layer, this is a very bad sign indeed and a leading indicator that the entire deal may be doomed. Staffing and selection, including the top team and retaining key talent, are the "canaries in the mine" test of whether you should stay or leave now. Any employee considering staying should be monitoring this throughout each stage of the deal.

There's another reason to keep an eye on what is happening with senior management. Often a change in CEO will mark the start of a reorganization of the company which includes a merger, acquisition, or sale. Sometimes this will be announced at the time of the appointment (where the CEO has been brought in specifically to "dress up" the company and sell it, for example, or when a new CEO is hired with acquisition experience), whereas other times there will be no public announcements but the changes being made indicate a possible acquisition or sale. Trying to interpret the latter may be difficult, but it is better to be prepared than surprised, especially when your job may depend on it.

CHAPTER 3

WHAT WILL HAPPEN TO ME NOW?

I deally, your boss would call you into a room just before the official announcement. He or she would tell you that your company is being acquired (or will be soon buying another company) and will explain what it means for the company and your department. You could then talk to someone from human resources (HR) about what it means for you personally and what options you have. There would be an internal website with more details as well.

That's the way it's supposed to work, but in the chaos surrounding an M&A deal, communication – or anything – rarely happens as it should. Often, the rumor mill works more efficiently than corporate processes and you may even know before your boss. Frequently, HR will be just as surprised as you and certainly will not yet know how to respond to the questions from the many staff members who all have one thought in mind: "What does this mean for me?" Often it is weeks or even months later that you find out whether you have a job or are being fired, what rights you have if you are being made redundant, and what departure package you may be offered.

IMPACT ON ALL EMPLOYEES

As shown in the last chapter, approximately 10% of the workforce can be expected to be made redundant when two companies combine. Specific deals may differ from this average, but very rare is the deal where no one is made redundant. Interestingly, even if your company is a target but the bidder then goes away, your job may still be at risk. For example, in 2000, after talks of merging with its larger competitor Deutsche Bank ended, Dresdner still announced plans to reduce headcount by 5000 employees or 10% of its workforce.

Thus, it can be said that all employees will certainly be at risk if their company is about to go through an M&A deal, and more so if their company is the target, as will be discussed later in the book. As will also be discussed later, this is true no matter at what level in the organization you are or how long you've been with the company. How you react after the announcement of the deal will be critical to your success in being retained by the company. But first look at what your boss – and other decision-makers – are thinking when the deal is announced, as their actions will clearly affect those who work closely with them.

WHAT WILL YOUR NEW BOSS BE THINKING?

Let's assume your manager did hear about the merger before the deal was announced publicly. The manager's thoughts will focus as well on whether his or her own job will be retained (and you can be certain that he or she *is* thinking first about this). Every manager also knows that although the newly announced deal – whether an acquisition or a merger – tells the market that the company is trying to expand, it also sends an immediate signal to competitors that all employees will be worried and are therefore easier to poach now than before.

According to consultants McKinsey & Co., "key employees usually receive inquiries within five days of a merger announcement – precisely when uncertainty is at its highest." If you are the acquiring company, despite the best efforts to conduct due diligence on the managers and staff of the target, and implement a process whereby you remain in control, you still may not even know who the key individuals are before they are contacted by headhunters or directly by competitors. It is a truism at the time of a deal announcement that the best employees (the sales people with the best clients, the most innovative product designer, the most efficient accountant, the most creative team in the R&D department, etc.) are the ones who will be the first to receive job offers externally. The most talented people are often as well known outside the company as inside. Your boss knows this too and should be taking immediate steps to make sure those he or she wants to retain will stay with the company.

"Walking the talk"

"As employees, we judge a company not by what leaders say but what they do, how they treat other people, how well they communicate, the actions they take to reassure the staff in the company which they have bought, and what sort of promises they make to retain you. All these (and many others) will send you messages about your new bosses and will help you decide whether your career will be best served by staying or by finding a new job.

"The way employees and potential employees see a company is sometimes called the employer brand, a perception that is made up of many factors. Organizations with a strong employer brand attract people to them. For example, Pret A Manger, a UK sandwich and coffee shop, attracts 4000 unsolicited applications to join them every month, so strong is its employer brand. On the other hand, a very well-known UK retail electrical discount chain's quality director once told me that they could never put the company's name on recruitment advertisements as they would never get any responses. No one wanted to work there.

"Let's look at this with an example contrasting two companies which set about the same task in two very different ways:

"In the 1990/1 recession, I was working for Y.J. Lovell Plc, a 200-year-old construction company. The recession hit us hard and suddenly I had to lay off over eighty staff. The chairman, an industry figurehead, Sir Norman Wakefield, said that we must carry out this unpleasant task in accordance with the company's tradition and long-established reputation as a great place to work. He said that in two years' time we would need these people back again and he wanted to ensure that they left Lovell feeling so good about the company that, when the time came, they would not hesitate to rejoin. Not only that, he said the way we treat these people is watched carefully by those who stay. We need them to feel really good about the company in a very difficult time. Accordingly, everyone was given free outplacement and, in most cases, they all found jobs in about six weeks. He was right; two years later, many of them were back in the company. The company still has a strong employer brand today.

"Contrast that to a similar situation in which I found myself almost 10 years later, in 2000. I was working for one of the world's most famous advertising agencies. We were taken over by a rival agency. Many of our people knew the rival's reputation as an employer and did not want to be in the newly merged company. From the day the takeover was announced in May to the date it was finalized in October, the morale of our people fell off a cliff and many employees sought jobs elsewhere. Naturally, with their eye off the ball, productivity fell and the business results were awful. By October, I was asked to make redundant 350 people in six European countries. With my Lovell experience in mind, my team and I set about this unpleasant task using the existing cultural norms, the basis for which were to protect our reputation as an employer in a marketplace known for its fickleness. We put in the plan outplacement for everyone, knowing that even if the business was doing badly now, in a year or so we would need to recruit. The accountants at our new owners ruled this out; they were not interested in people, merely costs. The message this sent to those who stayed was enormous and the staff turnover reached 34% (that is over one-third of the workforce) and cost the acquiring company £9 million that year.

"In a business depending on talent you need to look after the people you acquire in order to maintain business results."

Rowan Jackson, founder, Change Masters International

Best practice in selecting employees to remain in a newly merged company would see the top level (those reporting directly to the CEO) determined prior to public announcement of the deal and often communicated as part of that announcement or soon thereafter (as an example, see The Bank of New York/ Mellon merger below). This doesn't happen often enough in practice, but the principle remains: announce this level as quickly as possible to eliminate uncertainty in the external markets and within the two merging companies. Those executives at least can quickly begin to focus on the deal and on the important task of making sure other key employees are retained as they will not need to spend their time jockeying for position themselves, either internally or externally.

Spotlight: The Bank of New York/Mellon Financial

Merger of equals

On December 4, 2006, The Bank of New York and Mellon Financial Corporation announced a merger of equals. The press conference included a presentation that showed the board and first level of management: Tom Renyi of The Bank of New York would become executive chairman and oversee the merger integration with a view toward retiring within 18 months after the transaction was complete (he had announced his retirement well before the deal). Bob Kelly of Mellon would become chief executive and take on the chairman role when Tom retired. Of the 22 senior management positions reporting directly to the board, 15 were from The Bank of New York and seven from Mellon. The board would have 10 members from The Bank of New York and eight from Mellon.

In fact, senior management in most companies when faced with a merger or acquisition will begin to plan their team for the post-merger period as soon as they hear about the deal (assuming that they have decided to remain themselves). This process starts with a list of divisions or departments that are affected; some will have no overlap with the other company and it will not therefore have to be determined who to keep or who to fire. Just because there are no overlaps doesn't mean the employees are safe, however. Companies often sell off whole departments or divisions to help to pay for the deal.

Once the list of employees affected by the deal is compiled, management will ask questions such as, "What would happen if they left? Would we still be able to conduct our business? Could someone else do the same job as well or even better? Would any clients leave with the individual? How would other employees view their departure and would they then leave, too?" Asking these questions enables the transition teams to determine who the key individuals are. One clearly wants to be on that list!

Note as well that companies will often already have succession plans whereby they keep current a list of people who could do each key job in the company in case someone leaves unexpectedly or is promoted. In some companies, these succession plans are kept up to date with annual or semi-annual reviews, whereas in others they are only occasionally updated. When faced with a merger or acquisition, these succession plans are some of the first documents taken off the shelf and consulted. This allows management to make quick, informed decisions about whether an individual needs to be retained or could be replaced by someone else from a different part of the firm or, once the deal is announced, someone from the other company who can now be added to that succession list.

Although some companies with vast experience in conducting deals will have special teams on call to descend on their targets immediately after the announcement of the deal (see the example of Cisco below), most companies don't make acquisitions frequently enough for this. As noted in the previous chapter, after that first layer of management is announced around the time the deal is made public, it usually takes another six to eight weeks – at a minimum – to agree the next level, and each level beyond taking another six to eight weeks. Individual managers will often let their key team members know informally well before these formal announcements. They therefore hopefully avoid having their best people poached by their competitors or leave for other reasons. However, most employees are in a period of uncertainty during this time.

Spotlight: Cisco Systems Inc.

Integration process

Cisco is a serial acquirer and has been through periods when it would acquire up to 50 companies in a year. As a result, it has developed a standardized model for integration that has proven to be very effective.

A team drawn from all of its major departments determines if and how upper management and line-level employees fit into Cisco's structure.

As soon as the deal is completed, they send in their post-merger integration SWAT team. This is a team that exists permanently (or, in times of less frequent acquisition activity, can be assembled rapidly). As an information technology (IT) company, the IT team has particular relevance. For example, Cisco's IT team has a strict methodology for integrating all electronic mail, websites, product order systems, and telephone numbers into Cisco's systems. That and the other integration teams give each target pre-specified company information about Cisco, according to *ECCH Bulletin*.

The acquired company often becomes a discrete subdivision of Cisco so that key people are not lost to competitors. Personnel are integrated into Cisco immediately. The CEO of the acquired company is always appointed as a vice-president of Cisco Systems Inc. and most staff continue to report to him or her. All staff are offered stock options which acted as "golden handcuffs" to discourage them from leaving for competitors. The employees are immediately told their new positions, titles, and compensation packages. Importantly, no staff can be dismissed without the agreement of their vice-president (that is, their former CEO) and the Cisco CEO, but those who

> were made redundant usually find out very soon after the deal closes.
> The entire process was designed to take 100 days for the acquired company to be presented as part of Cisco, regardless of the size of the acquired company.

WHAT THEY REALLY MEAN

You just heard from your boss that your company will merge with another firm. One of the first things you need to do is to gather information. Clearly, listening to your boss is one key way to get some clarity about what's really happening. But you can't always rely on what he or she is saying because the deal may change, management themselves truly don't know, or senior managers may be trying to hide the truth from employees and the market.

Caution I: Runaway deal ahead

There's a danger in relying solely on the messages you get from management. You need to draw your own conclusions. Management may be caught up in events that have moved beyond their control – assuming they ever were in control. There are many deals which started off as bold yet safe strategic moves but that gathered a life of their own. These so-called "runaway deals" are like the proverbial runaway train that cannot be stopped as it barrels downhill: when the momentum of a deal takes charge, and executives and their advisors get embroiled in the detail and excitement of the transaction and therefore lose objectivity. A deal which should be stopped isn't, despite mounting evidence gathered during due diligence that it should be. Or a deal continues to make strategic sense, but not under the terms originally negotiated – and the parties are unable or unwilling to renegotiate the details of the deal, such as price. As a result, the company needs to make more redundancies than it intended – cutting not just fat, but muscle – in order to meet the financial expectations of external analysts and shareholders. In these cases, and all too often, the deal process itself becomes the manager, especially if the process hasn't been designed to allow for a decoupling from the deal once it is under way.

Of course, management and their advisors will hopefully try to avoid this problem. If they are following best practice, they are probably considering the following issues:

1. Understanding that in the early stages of the deal, there is only limited knowledge of the target
2. Building exit points into the deal process to allow for withdrawal from the deal at any stage
3. Allowing for adjustments to the deal
4. Publicizing details of the transaction only when they are certain
5. Trying to resolve as quickly as possible any ambiguities about the deal

Naturally, as can be seen from this list, it means that a well-managed deal assumes that there will need to be changes and adjustments; thus, any early communications about the specifics of the deal run a great risk of being inaccurate only because almost every deal does need to be changed in order to keep it on track. Thus, relying too heavily on the early information – even if accurate at the time – is dangerous. Just as the firms that are merging need to maintain some flexibility in order to merge successfully, so any individual wanting to remain in the firm also needs to reflect that flexibility.

Caution II: Management have no clue

The managers and advisors of the best-run deals understand that none will ever proceed exactly as planned. Yet plan they must.

As President Dwight Eisenhower said of his time leading the Allied forces in Europe in World War II, "In preparing for battle I have always found that plans are useless, but planning is indispensable." Among other reasons, he must have known that the very act of planning would enable him to react more swiftly once the battle situation shifted, just as M&A deal managers know that they will better be able to adapt to the unavoidable changes to a deal if they have planned properly and anticipated at least some of the possible scenarios where the deal can change.

But, as shown in the previous chapter, most deals are doomed to fail. Much of this failure is due to poor management after the deal closes, but it is linked to the decisions management made from the pre-announcement stage when the planning begins – or should begin – about what to do after closing. Managers with little experience or training in mergers and acquisitions – and those unwilling to call in advisors to assist – are also often unprepared for the complexity and chaos of a merger or acquisition.

Uncertainty in communications

"The first message to employees in our office was about the global integration which would bring big synergies; thousands of employees would be dismissed worldwide. People were in the position of extreme uncertainty for more than half a year. [The acquirer] didn't give information on who exactly they were going to keep and who they would fire. Communication was in the form of magic spells such as the phrase 'tremendous opportunities for everyone.' Even now this expression 'tremendous opportunities' brings negative memories. Nobody was convinced by these messages."

Treasury manager, consumer products company

Of course, one could say that management shouldn't enter into a deal that they don't understand and can't manage. True. But it happens too often. The failure rate of 60–70% of all deals attests to this.

Caution III: What managers don't want you to know

There are executives who are no longer in control of a deal and managers who never really had a clue about the merger. Yet there's a third category of manager: those who absolutely do know what's going on but do not want to reveal the details to others.

These executives may just be poor communicators (and this is probably evident in other non-M&A situations when the same managers have also not properly informed their staff and shareholders about critical strategic initiatives, such as a new product launch, entry into a new geographic market, or changes in senior management). Such managers may therefore not really intend to hide information from employees about the deal and may, if they were advised better or had more experience with deals, have disclosed critical information sooner and more accurately. They may not even understand that they have done anything wrong – they may not know that constant communication (once the deal is public) is critical to the success of the deal.

More likely, however, the executives are fully aware of the fact that they are keeping key facts from staff. They may even know about the need to communicate constantly with employees in order to keep control of the deal information flow, lessen employee stress, and reduce unwanted departures. It thus may be that they intentionally mislead those not in the inner circle because they must do this (for legal reasons because any disclosure would trigger a formal announcement or because the final decision about certain details of the deal haven't yet been decided) or just because they want to maintain control.

"Merger" and "acquisition" are often euphemisms for down-sizing which may explicitly be one of the strategies justifying the merger. Overlaps are inevitable: no company needs two CFOs or two heads of human resources, as mentioned earlier. Two sales departments are not needed. Why do they need two R&D groups? So perhaps the whole deal is driven by a desire to reduce headcount. Yet the deal is not yet completed and even if it is, the integration period remains, so people who ultimately will be redundant need to be retained for this period. Some firms will therefore (mis)lead their employees to believe that there will be few redundancies when in fact many are ultimately necessary. The redundancies will only be announced when management feel it is absolutely necessary for a particular group of employees to leave, and not one moment too soon, otherwise the employees may depart of their own accord and leave the firm exposed. Naturally, this is not good HR practice and there are other ways of retaining those soon-to-be-redundant employees (with the use of retention compensation packages, for example), but some firms will try to save that cost at the expense of the employees.

Misleading communication

"It was announced that nobody would be fired. That was true. Nobody was fired because the majority of people left by own intention."

Technical manager, manufacturing and sales

Thus, it is necessary for each employee to dig deeper and try to understand the underlying reasons why a deal is being done. If the industry is mature and has overcapacity, then it is likely that "merger" really means "mass firings." This was the case with the automobile industry in the 1990s when consolidation was taking place with deals such as Chrysler and Daimler Benz merging or around the same time in the oil industry when Exxon and Mobil merged, British Petroleum and Amoco, Chevron and Texaco, etc. The same occurred a decade later in the financial services industry with Bank of America acquiring Merrill Lynch, although other factors may have provided the catalyst for any of these deals.

Employees were often initially told that large-scale redundancies wouldn't be necessary – even when management knew that the promised synergies would require headcount reductions. Management hoped that "natural attrition" would take care of those required reductions. An employee who leaves voluntarily is one to whom no redundancy payments are necessary. The cost of firing an employee is substantial – and legislated for in many countries, as will be discussed later in this chapter. So, encouraging employees to resign voluntarily is often used to reduce the cost of the integration.

It could be all three

In any M&A deal, poor communication with staff may be due to all three factors above. Management may not be in complete control of the deal, they may just not understand everything that is taking place with the merger, and lastly because of these, may be reticent to communicate for fear of giving out wrong information (or conversely purposefully holding back information either for legal reasons or because they wish to be in control). Some of the types of common misleading communications are shown in Figure 3.1.

In virtually all deals, there *will* be some aspects of all of these, making it even more difficult for employees to filter out gossip and fiction from what's really happening. Thus, once again, it is

Beware of these phrases: understand what they really mean

"This is a merger of equals, not an acquisition"
- It is also often heard: "This is not an acquisition, it's the merger of two excellent organizations." But there is never a merger of equals even when the two companies are the same size based on *some* factors.
- This misconception of equality creates the impression and perhaps even the expectation that decisions will be made in some democratic or egalitarian fashion (such as who to make redundant, which systems to adopt and brands to retain, how to rationalize overlapping products, etc.).
- One company will be on top. Try to determine which one it is, as those who are in the "target" are at greater risk of redundancy.

"We will pick the best of both organizations"
- Although this is often the instruction from senior management, there is often a lot of ambiguity and therefore so much gray area in decisions about systems, processes, brands, products, suppliers, distributors, etc. Politics will play a role.
- A related statement is: "We will keep only the best, regardless from which organization." Don't believe it. The company may try to pick the best, but rarely can determine this. As one manager told us: " 'Best of Breed' is rubbish!"

"The right decisions about the new organization will take time"
- This phrase is often used even when the decisions have already been made or when senior management know that the process will be quick.
- This phrase is used to give the impression to those who will be redundant that they still have a chance. They may, but it will be slight.
- This phrase is also used to give the impression that the decisions about employee retention are objective, when actually there is necessarily a lot of subjectivity.
- Most experienced deal-makers know that decisions during merger integration can either be fast and painful or slow and painful; the former is naturally preferred. Therefore, they make decisions on 80% knowledge and don't wait for 100% certainty.

"Decisions about who will retain each job will be made on merit"
- As with all HR decisions – and despite the best of intentions as noted above – there must be some subjectivity. Politics plays an important role in the jockeying for power in the new organization.
- Employees should not believe statements which do not acknowledge this and, by stating it, the credibility of other important statements is called into doubt.

"No further acquisitions [or mergers] will be required"
- This is often said during a deal to give a sense (1) that this is the "deal to end all deals" and (2) if you stay with the company after this deal completes, then you don't need to worry about another such tumultuous reorganization interrupting your employment with the firm again. Of course this isn't true. Industries continue to change, and companies will have to change with them.
- Other deals will take place. In some industries and in some companies, these are frequent, whereas in others, they may go three or five years between deals. But deals will occur again, and the uncertainty about whether you have a job will once again raise its ugly head because of a pending M&A deal.

Figure 3.1   Misleading management communications

necessary for everyone in the two companies affected by the deal to look at what they can do to enhance their chances of being retained and not to rely too much on what they hear from others or from management.

SELECTING STAFF FOR REDUNDANCY

There will be formal processes put in place for this period when decisions are made about who will remain and who will go. Some acquirers are very clear in their intentions, whereas others appear uncertain and may truly not know at the time the deal is announced. True takeovers, and especially when the size of the target is much smaller than the acquirer, will normally see most if not all senior positions taken by the buyer; target company managers are either placed into lower level positions or asked to leave. When a deal is structured as a merger of equals (which actually doesn't happen very often), the two companies will try for some equality in appointing staff. See again the example above of The Bank of New York/Mellon merger, where there was an attempt at all levels to select staff and managers from both companies. In some cases in these mergers, two individuals will co-manage an area – ostensibly for the long term, but often in order for senior management to see who will shine and rise to the top.

It is not often the case that the best candidate for each position can be easily identified – especially as one goes lower and lower in the organization and there's less ability for an individual staff member to demonstrate how they are different or better than their peers. Certain individuals may be more likely to be retained because of their experience, tenure, or position, but most companies need to show a fair and rigorous process for selection.

Difficulty of choosing staff to retain

"Selecting staff to keep was like a Cold War negotiation between NATO and Warsaw Pact generals. No trust on either side. When the decision was made about who to keep and who to fire, it seemed like it was going to be similar to a prisoner swap through Checkpoint Charlie in Berlin: one from this side equals one from the other side, and it had to be even."

Vice-president, information technology, bank

The two most common methods of selection are described below:

- The *independent appraisal* process brings in one or more "neutral" outside organizations, usually human resources consulting firms, to appraise each candidate in interviews and 360° feedback sessions. All of the staff from both companies are appraised. The results of these appraisals are then discussed with the previously appointed more senior layer of management. Despite the obvious cost and time implications of running this process, it does provide employees with the appearance that the process is objective and independent, and not based on the cronyism or favoritism of an individual manager who would know people well from only one of the two organizations.

- The *post and invite* process starts with a listing ("posting") of each available position in the new organization and then employees from both companies are encouraged to apply for the positions. (Only if no one internal applies for a position is a search then conducted externally.) No one has a guaranteed position initially: all incumbents must also reapply for their current positions and if someone else thinks they can do that position better than an incumbent, then they are (in theory) considered equally with the incumbent. When this process has been used, it does create resentment among experienced managers who cannot understand why they must reapply for a position that is not changing much and that they may have held for many years. Yet it has the advantage of breathing some new life into the organization at all levels by allowing people to move into positions they wished they'd been able to move into previously; likewise, this process helps to eliminate "dead wood" (employees who have held a position for a long time but have not performed well).

In trying to determine who to keep and who to make redundant, many firms now also use psychometric testing and even intelligence tests. When the Royal Bank of Scotland acquired parts of ABN AMRO bank in 2008 after a hostile and protracted battle with Barclays Bank, they had an outside human resources consulting company interview every existing employee in some departments and even administered intelligence tests to all employees down to a certain level in the same areas in order to determine who would stay. Note that these were the staff from the acquirer and, if this were consistent with most deals, these employees should have felt as if they were in control. The process almost seemed to be designed to be stressful for those involved. From the interviews conducted for this book, other people from other acquirers also felt mistreated to the point where some who otherwise would have stayed with the company after the acquisition decided to leave.

Skill assessment

"Our group did different skills assessments and described our responsibilities. Our manager tried to highlight additional potential benefits of our work. He demonstrated the high value of our group to the new company. As a result, six people out of seven got an offer."

Logistics department project manager, consumer products firm

Both the above processes (with or without psychometric and IQ tests) are very time consuming; they also both assume that management are very clear about which positions they need to retain and fill, whereas in many mergers and acquisitions, the organizational structure is very fluid for many months as it properly needs to adapt to the uncertain and new corporate structure. Therefore, throughout the merger integration period, executives and other managers will be continually assessing who they want to keep in the new organization. The decision on who to retain can change during this period as well.

There will be wrong decisions. As one manager told us, "Everyone is so crappy during the merger process." Management are dealing with uncertain information about people they don't know very well in an organization that is changing and where the final structure is not yet known. That same manager described a deal where he said, "the good people were fired and the poor performers were the ones kept. This was due simply to bad management during the merger process." Another told us to "expect the worst," and be pleasantly surprised if the process actually does go well.

COMPANIES DO TRY TO KEEP EMPLOYEES AND BUDGET FOR THIS

During any period of significant organizational change such as a merger or acquisition, leadership is the most important driver of employee engagement (each employee's willingness and ability to contribute to the company's success). Naturally, having employees who agree with and support the merger are critical to the success of any M&A deal. During periods of transition and disruption such as happens during these deals, employees look first to leaders for guidance about how to react and behave, and for motivation and focus.

What leaders do during an M&A deal has a significant impact on how employees of both the acquirer and target react in terms of promoting a sense of community and purpose in the new organization. Positive employee perception of leaders is crucial to successful change whether in M&A deals or otherwise but, as both mergers and acquisitions represent such a significant amount of change for an organization, it is especially critical at the time of the deal and immediately thereafter. Employees want to believe that the company's leadership cares about them. When employees are convinced that leaders genuinely do care by observing that their actions are consistent with their talk, they become more open and willing to stick with the company through the chaos of the deal. They may even be eager to be part of what they consider to be an exciting new venture.

Most executives believe that they communicate well and often enough during M&A integrations to keep their workforces informed. However, information isn't enough. Engagement must be the minimum expected; excitement the goal. Research by Galpin and Herndon in 2006 suggested that the number one area of integration most needing improvement is communication. According to consultants McKinsey & Co., the management of the human side of change is the real key to maximizing the value of the deal, yet few resources tend to be allocated to communication, and most of that is focused externally rather than internally. Typically, executives are more concerned about discussing the changes to external customers and shareholders; communication to employees is often left to the HR department. This is usually unintentional and sends the wrong message to the very people who will be the ones to carry the company forward and will ultimately have the principal contact with customers.

When asked, most CEOs in the middle of a deal will acknowledge the importance of retaining key staff, yet their time, attention, and actions are focused elsewhere. It is therefore not surprising that employees feel under-appreciated and ill-informed during the deal process, thus causing many to leave at exactly the time when they should perhaps be concentrating on building a strong position in the newly merged company. Those who do find their own ways to get the correct information about the deal (which will be discussed in Chapter 9) will be at a distinct advantage to those who merely rely on the official channels of communication.

Because of this increased recognition in recent years that retained employees need more attention, there has been a trend toward changes in deals in the following areas. Knowing these will provide employees who stay with additional power to negotiate better terms and conditions for remaining with the company rather than jumping ship during the merger process:

- First, management will try to avoid or reduce redundancies because the full cost of making people redundant is now better known and it extends well beyond the headline cost of the required redundancy packages (and includes expensive items such as hiring temporary staff for interim coverage and the recruitment and training of new permanent staff).
- Second, management are now usually briefed to make sure that all redundancies are treated lawfully and fairly when they occur, thus avoiding adverse publicity, costly law suits, and negative impressions on those who remain with the company.
- Third, management will now often try to reduce the unavoidable but negative consequences of redundancy by offering outplacement (professional career and personal support) to those who leave. They also will sometimes offer such assistance even to those who remain with the company.

Managements usually do try to reduce the number of people being made redundant. From the acquirer's perspective, this means conducting a very careful assessment of the actual number of layoffs necessary, but at the same time being aware that multiple rounds of redundancies may be even worse than making too many people redundant in the first round (see the examples later in this chapter regarding Daimler/Chrysler and BASF/Boots Pharmaceutical).

Employees can be proactive as well and may be able to ask for some protective measures in their employment contracts. One example of such protective measures would be the so-called "golden parachutes" for senior management, "silver parachutes" for middle management, and even "tin parachutes" when extended to all employees (such as were in place at Mellon Financial at the time of the aforementioned merger in 2007 with The Bank of New York; these "tin parachute" protections were given to all employees following a previously unsuccessful hostile takeover attempt by The Bank of New York). Such "parachutes" normally provide for a level of compensation well above the statutory minimum in case of a takeover.

THE ROLE OF THE HUMAN RESOURCES DEPARTMENT IN DEALING WITH STAFF

A common finding of many previous studies – and certainly confirmed in my own experience and interviews – has been that human resources issues receive too little attention, are unmanaged, and are often neglected – thus seriously affecting the success of M&A deals. This seems to be due in part to a belief that people issues are soft, and therefore hard to manage (certainly in contrast to the financial aspects of a deal that appear accurate to several decimal places). In many corporate boardrooms, there is still a general lack of awareness or consensus that the people issues below the top management layers are critical to the success of a merger or acquisition. Of course, M&A deals are always chaotic, changing, and complex, so often focus is diverted elsewhere towards what appear at the time to be more critical issues, such as retaining clients and deciding which products to keep. Time and resource pressures prevent the proper focus on the people side of the business. But no matter the reason, it is clear that in many deals, the human side is often overlooked.

As the merger of two companies will almost always result in employment casualties, a key role of the human resources function is to minimize the impact of these casualties, not just on those being made redundant but, perhaps more importantly from the organization's perspective, on those who remain. HR must work to alleviate staff anxieties but also develop a "key personnel" retention policy. Some companies recognize this and claim that the retention of key talent is their first concern in any of their acquisitions. General Electric is often cited in this regard, as well as Cisco, the subject of a Spotlight case study earlier in this chapter.

Traditionally, HR professionals came to M&A deals relatively late, so it was difficult for them to have much impact on the process itself. Their entry into the deal typically started at the time or even just after the deal was announced. They had limited involvement pre-announcement, and the lack of success on human resources issues reflected this late involvement.

However, research suggests that companies are learning from their mistakes. A Tower Perrin survey in 2004 entitled *HR Rises to the Challenge* suggested an increase in HR involvement in the due diligence (during the pre-closing) phase of deals from 39% in 2000 to 62% in 2004. As it is the due diligence phase that really digs into the actual operations of the target company including an understanding of its personnel, this is a critical phase in which to have increased HR involvement. This increase is an encouraging trend. Other studies confirm this continuing improvement in the use of HR earlier in deals, although it should also be noted that one reason for the jump in human resources due diligence involvement is the surge in underfunded pension liabilities, which has become a significant issue in a number of recent M&A transactions and has caused several high profile deals to be called off, including a bid for the UK retail bookshop W.H. Smith. Typically, this is more a finance than people issue, so if earlier HR involvement is only related to an investigation of pension liabilities, it doesn't necessarily mark an improvement in the handling of other individual employee concerns.

Being involved earlier in the process allows the HR function to influence key decisions that affect the success of integration activities much later in the deal process. Despite this, there remains a significant gap between recognizing that people are important to the deal and actually taking action to manage the issues raised. HR involvement earlier in the deal process isn't effective if it isn't linked with an ability to restructure that process to reflect employees' needs.

People issues should be considered right from the point when initial planning starts during the pre-announcement stage. This is to make sure that the M&A process protects and enhances the portion of the value of the deal that comes from the people in an organization. However, the 2004 study above by Towers Perrin found that just 26% of the companies surveyed considered their HR departments to be fully ready to aid a merger or acquisition effort. There is a clear problem for the organization – and deal – if senior executives don't feel their HR departments are qualified to advise on M&A employee issues. And if they are concerned, you should be too!

When a target is being openly considered, employees will be anxious about whether they will be kept or not. As a result, during the due diligence process most managers and employees will and should try very hard to be seen as being cooperative. Others will try to hold onto key pieces of information for as long as possible in order to maintain their control as well as to enhance their perceptions of being indispensable to the organization where "knowledge is power" and they think such power is even greater if you are the only person who controls or understands that knowledge.

It is also critical during this due diligence process that information is not hidden. One deputy director of finance warned us about how dangerous it would be during this period for an employee to try to hide the negative things about their job or work, including potential problems. The whole due diligence process in many M&A deals is very extensive, often with a large number of external experts crawling around both companies looking for buried or hidden problems. In most cases, management are also more diligent than at any other time in an organization's life in digging into the two companies to determine what is really happening. Regulators and major shareholders may be looking deeply into the company as well.

Once the deal is announced, communication with staff (and externally) should be timely and continuous, but it doesn't always happen. This is especially important on the topic of redundancies, as demonstrated by an example given to us from Procter & Gamble's acquisition of Gillette in 2005. One of the first announcements about that deal was about the synergies expected from the global integration of the two companies, which would result in an estimated 6000 employees being dismissed worldwide. But for more than half a year, employees in some areas didn't know who would get an offer to stay. This uncertainty caused many to leave, some to competitors who were naturally aware of the situation within the two companies.

Senior managers with the responsibility of designing the new organization will usually try to make informed and fast decisions about who should be kept and who should be fired. When making these decisions from the firm's perspective, both speed and precision are extremely important. But, as noted earlier, individual managers and employees also need to and will focus first on their own futures, which will distract and slow down the corporate processes. People become risk averse in their job because making a mistake for the company at this time can be extremely costly not just for the company, but also for the individual – and at a time when maintaining an excellent reputation vis-à-vis your peers is critical. Nevertheless, although the decision process should be as quick and smooth as possible to keep anxiety at a minimum

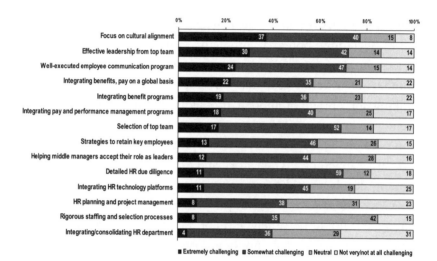

Figure 3.2 Most challenging people issues in M&A deals

Source: Towers Perrin, *HR Rises to the Challenge: Unlocking the Value of M&A* (2004), reproduced with permission

and to maintain employee commitment to the maximum, it doesn't always happen this way.

Towers Perrin also found that there were many other people issues on the minds of senior management during an M&A deal. These range, as shown in Figure 3.2, from very critical and sometimes narrow issues such as pay, benefits, roles, and performance systems through to much more difficult and broad issues such as leadership and communication. Handling all of these simultaneously does require a sophisticated and experienced HR team with strong leadership. Often outside consultants are brought in to assist as well.

Senior managers will need to reassure those left behind that they have made the right decision to stay with the company. Each employee who remains will have to be told their specific job role and title. They need to know that they will receive good remuneration packages with, if applicable, performance-related bonuses.

The future strategy of the new organization and each individual department needs to be communicated so that employees "buy into" the new culture and business and work to support it fully.

Some employees must be retained for the transition period, but will not be needed once the integration of the two companies is complete. For example, the two merging companies may have two different accounting systems, but ultimately only one will be used. Initially, when the companies are combined, both systems will be required as accounts will still need to be prepared for all parts of the newly combined company but some of the newly acquired divisions will not have had time yet to change to the other company's system. During this transition period, accountants and IT support team personnel will be needed from both companies to run the old "legacy" systems, but eventually one group will no longer be needed. Thus, they will have to be given incentives to stay with the company until that period is over. The communications, compensation, and benefits for these employees need to be directed at the full length of their remaining term of employment, so as to build the trust and commitment required for that length of time and leave as good an impression as possible. This "good impression" is necessary as these employees could be a supplier or client in the future, or potential re-hires, and they certainly will be talking to the other employees who are retained for the long term.

To do this properly, there must be effective communications: from the firm's perspective, speaking to all employees directly, making intentions clear, and reassuring them can buy much needed loyalty, time, and credibility. The second and third tiers of management should not be neglected, but often are. One of the unfortunate facts about mergers and acquisitions is that most of the target's senior management will leave within two or three years, as noted in the first chapter. Exceptions exist, but are less frequent than expected. From the individual's perspective, each manager and employee will need to assess whether they believe what they're being told, and the impact on them personally. This requires a certain degree of personal business intelligence gathering and social networking (see Chapter 9).

Spotlight: Daimler/Chrysler

Delayed redundancies

In a joint press release at the time of their merger in 1997, the president of Daimler-Benz, Jürgen Schrempp, and the president of Chrysler, Robert Eaton, declared that "there will be no plant closures or layoffs as a result of the merger." However, in 2000, the company announced there would be between 20 000 and 40 000 job cuts in the North American Chrysler division. Schrempp, by then the DaimlerChrysler president, claimed that the company was overstaffed by at least 6%.

However, this overstaffing was due to an excess of employees following the merger of 1997. This could have been anticipated, would have been more honest with employees, and was anyway commonly known and predicted at the time of the merger, at least by most external analysts.

Announcing redundancies two or three years after the initial deal can cause even greater stress to the employees who thought that they were survivors. Employees are better prepared to handle the bad news straight after the transaction than two years later, after the newly merged culture has started to take shape and when they thought they could rely on management's assurances regarding the merger, often accompanied, as in the above Daimler/Chrysler example, with promises of no further redundancies.

Other companies have suffered similar employee disenchantment, such as when the Knoll Pharmaceuticals division of the German company BASF AG acquired Boots Plc's pharmaceutical division in the UK in 1995, and had not just a second round of redundancies (after assurances that there would be only one), but a third.

As discussed earlier in this chapter, a cynic might be tempted to say that sometimes the poor HR processes during an M&A deal are intentional: senior management know that they want to reduce headcount and it is cheaper if employees leave voluntarily than if the company has to make them redundant and give them a large separation package, often required by law or contract. This could be the case in some deals, but unfortunately, if this is true, it would likely backfire on the company because, as noted earlier, it is probable that the best people in the company are the ones who will leave first as they typically have the greatest number of external opportunities. Such a process would also affect the ability to integrate the two companies.

Spotlight: Procter & Gamble/Gillette

A process designed to cause employees to leave?

From the perspective of many employees interviewed (including some who remained with the firm) the complex and sluggish decision-making process at P&G slowed down the pace of integration when it purchased Gillette in 2005. But the most critical factor cited in interviews that served as a reason for employee resignations was the way in which the HR policies were applied during the acquisition.

In some divisions where there were significant overlaps, the Gillette employees were offered lower positions or those with less responsibility than they had previously held. In addition, there were other changes to their employment terms in order to bring them in line with the P&G policies:

- Bonuses were incorporated into fixed salaries (which especially affected the former Gillette sales department).
- Slower career growth was explicitly indicated, attributed to the larger size of the new organization and the large numbers of employees who had relevant experience for each position.
- Greater segregation of duties, which led to much narrower job scope and lower job enrichment for many who previously held positions with more responsibilities.
- P&G's policy of recruiting only at the entry level would prevent future filling of open senior positions with qualified personnel, and more of these open senior positions were expected because of departures as a result of the acquisition.

P&G thus failed to retain many Gillette employees. A number of former employees commented that the company didn't seem to be too bothered about the fact that so many people were leaving since the main goal appeared to be to get the new Gillette brands on board and expand the business through the new customer reach while simultaneously achieving cost synergies through, among other things, lower employee expense.

COACHING

Employers may provide career coaching for some or all employees. Consider yourself lucky if you have this benefit currently, as it is not yet common (career coaching may be more common in some large organizations in banking and consulting, especially at the senior management levels in those firms). It may be possible for you to request such a coach even before a deal is announced or even contemplated.

The primary focus of most company-sponsored executive coaching is to improve the employee's actions and career within their current organization. When a merger or acquisition is announced, the coaching needs to shift to a much broader consideration of career, as external as well as internal possibilities must be considered. If you do have an executive coach, the time during the merger process can be an important time for the coach to assist with a firmer and more objective understanding of your personal strengths which can be used beyond the current organization. If you have been working with an executive coach before the deal announcement, you should hopefully feel more secure about your personal capabilities and view redundancy in a much different and less stressful way.

Most will not already have a career or executive coach. During a merger or acquisition, there has been a growing trend for companies to offer the services of such a coach on a temporary basis, called an outplacement coach if used explicitly during this period for someone being made redundant. Because of the number of deals taking place, as discussed in the previous chapter, almost any professional employee should consider themselves at risk and ask for such coaching. Many companies already provide this counseling support through their employee assistance programs or similarly provided benefits, but it is usually up to the employee to initiate its use.

THE LEGAL FRAMEWORK

Employees may not be aware that the law in most countries provides them with statutory protections in case of redundancy. These can be significant. For example, in the USA at the time this book was written, if a company has at least 100 workers, then it must follow the federal Worker Adjustment and Retraining Notification Act (WARN). This Act requires, among other things, that the company provides notification to the affected workers 60 calendar days in advance of plant closings and mass layoffs. Employees entitled to notice under WARN include managers and supervisors, as well as hourly-paid and salaried workers, not counting those who have worked less than six in the last 12 months or those who work an average of less than 20 hours a week. According to the US Department of Labor, it is intended to give "workers and their families some transition time to adjust to the prospective loss of employment, to seek and obtain other jobs, and, if necessary, to enter skill training or retraining." Individual states in the USA have additional laws and regulations covering redundancies.

The requirement for legal protections

"Since the merger, I am aware now that it is a numbers game and that personal skills/experience are not important. The whole 'selection' process is a legal necessity rather than good business practice."

Sales supervisor and team leader, telecoms firm

Employees should know that they can remind their managers that the onus should be on the organization to take redundancy issues seriously during a merger. Redundancy policies should be built into the employment contract along with other company benefits, the code of conduct, and other legal parts of the contract. This will give the employer an opportunity to prepare employees for any changes and let employees know their rights; it assists in providing a process that will be perceived as fair and consistent.

Different countries have different statutory requirements for compensation, consultation periods, non-cash compensation, and so on. In Europe, for example, it is generally accepted that there are more legal restrictions on a company making redundancies in many countries on the Continent than in the UK. For a company making an acquisition of a firm that operates throughout Europe but where redundancies must be made, often the initial round of redundancies will occur in the UK with its more flexible labor laws than in, say, Germany or France where there are greater requirements for consultation with works councils and where the legal minimum for redundancy packages is greater than in the UK. Globally, many consider the USA to be a location where there are fewer cultural barriers to redundancy because someone with a history of being made redundant is not "marked for life" as being a problem employee, which may be the case in, say, Japan.

If redundancy policies are clear even before redundancies are necessary or announced, you will know your rights and thus have a more open relationship with your employer at the time of a merger when they do take place. Such openness benefits the company as well: as many acquisitions are unsolicited, this process builds goodwill among employees in case senior management need to have their support in rejecting an unwanted bid.

Redundancies are the acid test of employer/employee relationships

"I think that you only really find out how good a firm is when they make you redundant. It's all very well firms claiming they are 'Employers of Choice,' but it is only how they treat you on exit that you know how good they really are."

Reader comment in Here is the City, *a London-based news and careers website*

The 2002 Chartered Institute of Personnel and Development redundancy survey mentioned in Chapter 1 found that the majority of employers (72%) paid redundancy compensation above the statutory level, 50% provided employment counseling such as the outplacement coaching mentioned above, and 44% provided access to outplacement agencies, which are organizations that help soon-to-be ex-employees with lists of companies that are hiring. This is encouraging, but the starting point is the statutory minimum, as all redundancies must be treated in a lawful and fair manner. Generally, in many if not most countries the legal framework for redundancy consists of the following:

- Payment of compensation for the job loss ("redundancy pay")
- Protection against unfair selection
- Requirement for consultation

Other statutory rights may be provided in some countries, such as the required involvement of works councils and specified treatment of certain individuals who might suffer discrimination, such as older workers and women.

Redundancy pay

Despite being critical to the ultimate success of the deal, the compensation and benefits implications of a merger are often not considered early enough. The planners and designers of the deal tend to place compensation and benefit considerations far down the priority list and way below issues such as the price paid for the target and who will comprise the leadership team in the newly combined organization. When employees are considered, the focus in these high level planning sessions is normally on those who will be made redundant (as they must be given departure packages immediately), not those who actually mean more to the organization – those who are staying on. To some degree, those remaining are "taken for granted," which is exactly the opposite of what should take place.

The process of analyzing benefit packages ideally should be conducted before the deal is announced and perhaps even before the ultimate price for the target is finalized. This would reduce the risk of identifying a gap in benefits between the two companies so large that they cannot be harmonized or where the expenses will be particularly high and could affect the cost of the deal. Because this is often not done, a great deal of uncertainty remains in the minds of the employees who are leaving, those who wish to stay, and those who are still trying to decide what to do.

The legal minimum payment for redundancy differs from country to country. For example, in the UK, redundancy payments are based, among other things, on the age of a person and the length of service with the company. In other countries, the law may be more specific. For example, statutory rules in Russia state that the employee is entitled to two months' pay regardless of tenure and, furthermore, if an employee cannot find a job in the first two months after being laid off, another month's salary must be paid. In the USA, statutory requirements differ by state but typically are lower than the two examples above, as many states have "right to work" laws that allow employees to be fired without much proof of the need to do so by the employer.

These laws are subject to change at any time, of course, and any employee facing redundancy should check on what applies to them. A quick internet search should give some idea of the current laws covering redundancy, but legal advisors will have the most up-to-date information and the most experience in providing assistance if required.

> ### Seriously consider a redundancy package
>
> "What would I have done differently? I would seriously consider taking the redundancy offered and moving on."
>
> *Vice-president, insurance industry*

Protection against unfair selection

In most countries, the selection criteria which can or must be used in a redundancy situation have not been defined by law. However, employers are usually required to follow agreed procedures, and criteria for selection cannot directly or indirectly discriminate on factors that would otherwise be prohibited such as race, religion, disability, age, sex, sexual orientation, marital status, etc. Selection criteria should be clearly stated in a redundancy policy that is available for all employees to see and should be applied in an unbiased manner. This is why external consultants are often used for this process, as noted earlier, because they may protect the company from accusations of bias. The selection criteria most often used are based on the assessment of performance, skills, absence record, and tenure with the company.

The most common criterion for redundancy assessment is performance, based on the application of relevant skills. A "skills matrix" is usually created, which scores (sometimes using self-administered tests and other times by conducting 360° assessments) each of the key relevant skills necessary to perform well in the post-merger position, including client focus, quality of work, external and internal qualifications required, and flexibility. These assessment tools and selection criteria are only part of the process: the CIPD redundancy practices survey noted in the first chapter indicated that in 85% of organizations, line managers were involved in selecting employees for redundancy. These tools are inputs to, but not full determinants of, the decision as to which people will be retained or made redundant. This is a critical point that will be highlighted later: do not forget that even the most objective-looking redundancy process will include a large subjective element. Ultimately, in most companies there will be an opportunity for management to make its own decisions regardless of the results of these skills matrices, independent assessment interviews, and other selection tools.

These selection methods are not mutually exclusive; they can be used in combination with each other. Usually, the employer has only to show reasonable care in identifying and applying selection for redundancy objectively.

One bank's selection process

"We sat round a table with some of their management team and decided who we needed. We then had to find a way of making the ones we didn't either leave or realize they were no longer needed. With hindsight we could have done it better, as the good ones left anyway."

Finance director, support services, bank

Requirement for consultation

There is also a requirement for consultation between employers and employees. In some countries there are thresholds in terms of numbers of employees so that above a certain number, there are additional requirements on consultation (for example, in the UK, this is the case with more than 20 people being made redundant at one time; note the aforementioned level of 100 employees in the USA). In companies where there are independent trade unions or employee works councils representing staff, these may act on behalf of certain employee groups. They may need to be informed earlier in the process than in companies where no such worker representation exists. There are other countries, such as Germany, where employee representatives sit on the advisory board of companies; these representatives will naturally have been aware of the merger negotiations from an early stage in most cases.

From the perspective of the employee, consultation can be very helpful. The requirement to have someone discuss the redundancy with you does provide you with someone who will listen to what you have to say, someone who may provide moral support and understanding, and someone who understands the redundancy process and your rights. This can help to minimize the damage redundancy may cause, especially in terms of self-confidence and the ability to find alternative employment quickly.

Consultations should occur when redundancy proposals are still at the formative discussion stage and you have reasonable time to consider its implications and respond with an informed decision. At a minimum, the information that needs to be provided should include the proposed selection criteria for redundancy, the reason for the redundancies, the proposed compensation package, and the total number of employees that are to be made redundant, including those that are in the same situation as you (with assurances that all are being treated equally).

Psychological contracts

Perhaps as important as the legal employment contract for many employees will be the implied "psychological contract," as has been described by a number of researchers and observers of employees in M&A situations. According to Denise Rousseau, who first wrote about the concept in 1996, there exists a psychological contract between each employee and his or her organization. Victoria Bellou, who conducted a broad survey of employees in 2007, noted that psychological contracts appear "when an employee believes that a promise of future returns has been made, a contribution has been given and thus, an obligation to provide future benefits has been created." Different aspects of this psychological contract include the opportunities for promotion, appropriate salaries, pay according to performance, continuous education, long-term employment, personal development, support for personal problems, interesting work, involvement in decision making, and recognition for a job well done. Psychological contracts are held by individuals, but are subjective, subject to change, and often based on emotions.

Psychological contracts assume that each party – both the employee and employer – knows and has certain expectations of the other. If employees in the organization are treated as they expect to be treated, then the company will have in return a workforce that is highly motivated, loyal, and committed to the firm. But a radical change such as a merger or acquisition can break the contract in the mind of the employee or, from the company's perspective, be the cause to make major changes to or even terminate the psychological contract as it existed. As a consequence, the psychological contract will need to be re-established, which may involve a degree of "renegotiation" and adjustment from both sides. As psychological contracts are not formal legal documents, it may be unclear until the culture solidifies many years later what this informal contract really includes. It may therefore be difficult for any employee to decide their own fate – assuming they have a choice – at the time of the merger. This becomes yet another stressful situation for the employee and one over which the typical employee will feel that he or she has little control.

Worst case legal scenarios

Despite the company's best efforts (and let's give most companies the benefit of the doubt that they are trying to treat their employees properly and legally), mistakes can be made in the redundancy process. In this case, you do have legal recourse: depending on your situation, you may have access to managers above those who have treated you wrongly in order to appeal, there may be a formal process set up during the acquisition to handle such problems (these are often well publicized in the official merger communications), your company may have an internal employee assistance program that can help, or you can hire an external employment lawyer or solicitor to sue (or threaten to sue) the company. For any of these, you should be advised early in the process of appeal whether your particular case is likely to be successful.

In case you need to bring in a lawyer ...

"Keep meticulous notes of all discussions with dates, even if they are 'round the coffee machine' talks."

General manager, professional services firm

These "worst case scenarios" almost guarantee that you will want to leave the company, which is difficult for any employee but especially one who has previously worked hard to maintain their position. These formal and legal recourses should be used as a last resort, but it is useful to know throughout the process that these options do exist.

NOW WHAT?

This chapter makes the whole redundancy process sound very clinical and emotionless. The opposite, however, is true. Finding out that your company is going to be acquired or substantially changed through a merger or acquisition can be traumatic or exciting, depending on where you expect to be once the dust has settled. The chapter that follows will show how employees typically react to the announcement of a deal, whether they are informed of their statutory rights or not, whether the selection criteria for redundancy were perceived to be fair or not, and regardless of whether the company has effectively communicated why the deal has been done in the first place.

CHAPTER 4

HOW WILL I FEEL?

Perhaps the initial reaction of some employees to finding out about their company being acquired or being an acquirer is one of goodwill and cooperative spirit, if not even excitement. Typically, the message from the CEO will be full of very positive forward-looking statements about how wonderful the deal will be for employees of both companies, their clients, and shareholders. This attitude may be sincere from these senior executives who worked on the deal and think that they have a job in the newly combined and soon-to-be-larger company. For most employees, however, any initial enthusiasm will quickly dissipate when the reality hits that the fine print about the deal includes significant layoffs in the workforce.

Employees will naturally be anxious upon hearing about a merger and during the integration. Even if not fearful of losing their job (and actually everyone – even the CEO – should be worried), there will be concerns as to whether compensation, job security, role, and other employment benefits will be reduced. But the most common first reaction is one of shock, and a person in shock is not able to think rationally and clearly about the situation.

Spotlight: CGU/Norwich Union

Initial reaction to a deal announcement

"I'm scared. I haven't been here very long. I was made redundant from another company – and now this!" said a worker to the BBC at Norwich Union in 2000 when it was announced that it would merge with another insurance company. The union leader said, "I've spoken to young people there today, and they are dismayed and shocked. Very little work is being done in the office at the moment. People will be more intent on finding out what the implications are for them personally."

EMPLOYEES AND STRESS

M&A deals are change events which signify a massive interruption in the professional and private lives of everyone in the two companies that are merging. Both the uncertainty associated with the event and the actual changes it brings can cause not just shock but also fear, anxiety, and stress. The architects of the deal may think of it principally as a financial transaction or a way to grow the business, but to the employees involved, the merger or acquisition represents a significant and potentially emotional and stressful series of life events on par with other events, such as retirement, marriage, or a divorce.

At best, you will likely experience a change in job, which according to the Holmes and Rahe stress scale (see Figure 4.1), first developed in 1967, is the 18th most stressful event for most people; at worst, you will lose your job (#8 on the scale). Both

Life event	Life change units
1. Death of a spouse	100
2. Divorce	73
3. Marital separation	65
4. Jail term	63
5. Death of a close family member	63
6. Personal injury or illness	53
7. Marriage	50
8. Dismissal from work	47
9. Marital reconciliation	45
10. Retirement	45
11. Change in health of family member	44
12. Pregnancy	40
13. Sexual difficulties	39
14. Gain of a new family member	39
15. Business readjustments	39
16. Change in financial state	38
17. Death of a close friend	37
18. Change to a different line of work	36
19. Change in number of arguments with spouse	35
20. Major mortgage	32
21. Foreclosure of mortgage or loan	30
22. Change in responsibilities at work	29
23. Child leaving home	29
24. Trouble with in-laws	29
25. Outstanding personal achievement	28
26. Spouse starts or stops work	26
27. Begin or end school	26
28. Change in living conditions	25
29. Revision of personal habits	24
30. Trouble with boss	23
31. Change in work hours or conditions	20
32. Change in residence	20
33. Change in schools	20
34. Change in recreation	19
35. Change in religious activities	19
36. Change in social activities	18
37. Minor mortgage or loan	17
38. Change in sleeping habits	16
39. Change in number of family reunions	15
40. Change in eating habits	15
41. Holidays	12
42. Minor violation of law	11

Figure 4.1 Holmes and Rahe stress scale

Source: *Journal of Psychosomatic Research*, Volume 11, 1967

would be exacerbated by being combined with the 15th and 22nd most stressful events (a major business adjustment and a change in work responsibilities) and could also be combined with a change in financial situation (#16), a change in living conditions (#28), trouble with your boss (#30), and a change in working hours or conditions (#31). As a score of over 150 for a 12 month period is indication of a moderate risk of stress-related illness, it is not surprising that shock will be an employee's first reaction to the announcement of a merger or acquisition.

PERSONAL CONCERNS

During the earliest stages of a merger or acquisition once people are aware of what is happening, the first topic to become a matter of great concern among people at all levels of the organization, from executives to junior employees, is the personal uncertainty – often called the "me issues." Before people start thinking about what the acquisition means from a business perspective, they consider the impact on them, personally.

Worried stiff

"I was recently made redundant. The worry of it was far worse than when the axe fell. I've actually found that a big relief, as I feel that I can now get on with my life."
Reader comment in Here is the City, *a London-based news and careers website*

When any deal is announced, employees are likely first to relate it to any prior experience, if any, they have had with mergers or acquisitions (those experiences probably having been unsatisfactory) and second to relate it to the widespread coverage in the press of large M&A deals – many get front page coverage when announced, often with the headline screaming out the number of redundancies to be made. This will also cause many employees to be angry, concerned about potential job loss and role changes, uncertain, and dissatisfied with the way that management are communicating with them. Specifics about the deal will be scarce, except to those who were "insiders" during the planning and negotiation, and who likely already know how they will be treated in the new company. For the rest, there are more questions than answers. Employees whose psychological contract (see Chapter 3) is more transactional – that is, they see the company fulfilling its obligation to them by paying them – will ask different questions than those whose psychological contract with the company is emotional and who feel that its bonds include social relationships as well. The former will be asking about compensation arrangements, for example, while the latter may be more concerned about how their close colleagues are being treated.

Target company employees especially will be asking such questions as: "Who are these new owners? What are their real intentions? Can we trust what they say? Do we still have jobs, and will they be the same as before? Why did our previous owners sell? Did we contribute to the need to sell out, or did management just betray us?" The answers are likely to come first from the rumor mill.

Since acquisitions are normally very expensive with a large premium paid to the target (on average, usually between 20% and 40% higher than the company's value before the purchase was announced), it is almost certain that one component of the deal will be to reduce costs. On the upside for those who remain with the newly combined company, the acquisition may generate greater prospects for development, career enhancement, and the opportunity to change boss. But to most employees, the fear of losing a job looms larger than any potential new opportunities afforded by the deal.

These personal concerns will be common not only among the employees of the target company but also among those of the acquirer. It is unlikely that anyone from either company comes through the experience entirely unscathed or without a tale to tell. Almost everyone will have experienced at least one of the stress items in the above Holmes and Rahe stress scale. The number of people eager to share with us their experiences is just one piece of evidence for that!

When they hear about a proposed deal, employees often shift their loyalties from the company to themselves. Prior to the announcement of the merger, they identified with the company: for example, when asked by friends about their day, it would be discussed in terms of what they did at work and for the company. After the deal announcement, the focus turns on themselves: the same question will elicit an answer of "I've been trying to figure out what I should do next, either leave or stay, and if I stay, I'm looking at this or that possible new position." This change often causes employees to shift away from company-specific training (such as learning how to use a new system) to developing portable skills of benefit principally to themselves (interviewing skills, for example).

SHIFTING EMOTIONS

In general, after hearing about a deal, one moves emotionally through three phases, with each phase having several steps (see Figure 4.2). Upon hearing the news that their company is being acquired (or that perhaps it is merging or making the acquisition), the typical employee will soon start looking at the change *negatively*, expecting that things will get worse and not yet able to see how it might be better for them or the company. They are focused on the "ending" of their previous job or even company. Then, after further reflection, discussion with others, and some more accurate information, the negative feelings stop, but usually

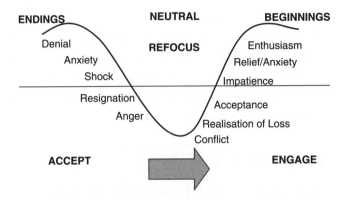

Figure 4.2 Change curve – "we versus them" to "us"
Source: C. Benham, ACHA, reproduced with permission (concept originally developed by Elisabeth Kübler-Ross, 1969)

only to the degree that the employee remains *neutral*. Most are in a state where they want the company to show them how it could be better, but not yet accepting that it will be. Eventually, unless they have opted to leave the firm either voluntarily or involuntarily, they begin to believe that it will get *better* both for themselves and the company overall. This marks the "beginning" of commitment to the new company for those who will remain.

Different individuals, even in the same company and division, will move through these phases at different paces. These phases do not relate directly to the stages of a deal shown earlier in Chapter 2 which correspond to the actions of the company and not necessarily its employees. Some individuals may come to grips with the potential of the deal – moving from denial to enthusiasm very quickly after the deal is announced because they can see the potential for the company and themselves of such a deal. Others will still be grieving the loss of their old company years after it has ceased to exist, never really accepting that the new organization has the same potential for them or their colleagues as the old one did.

The first step of personal transition is *denial* – when a person cannot believe that their company will be truly changed to such a degree and additionally refuses to believe that redundancy may happen to them and perhaps to many of their friends and colleagues. This denial is a temporary separation from reality wherein there is some refuge from the stress and pain of the situation and, therefore, relief from psychological tension. This initial reaction is followed by feelings of anxiety and shock, with all three of these emotions often mixed together.

What I felt when I heard the news ...

"My general feeling could be described as nervousness and anxiety. People were worrying about their future careers. People's feelings regarding the acquisition were developing ... a sharp rise of anxiety right after the announcement of the acquisition, then followed by a decline in anxiety when people realized that they couldn't do anything particular at that moment, and then an increase in anxiety again when some new information became available, etc."

Local head of IT, consumer products company

After the time in denial, a person will be resigned to the fact that the deal will proceed and then often enters a period of *anger* and feeling of the unfairness of the situation. Self-image at this stage is very vulnerable. Furthermore, an individual at this point blames others for the potential redundancies that will happen in the attempt to minimize the reality of the situation. This is a time of conflict when the organization and senior management are blamed for what is happening.

There's a pull to the old but also from the new that causes anger eventually to decrease because next begins a period when an employee starts to realize fully what has actually happened, and feels both despair and loss. There is no willingness yet to start a job search if the greatest fear is redundancy, but employees at this time are on the cusp of finally accepting that maybe it might be better. They can choose to be part of it or leave. Of course, the choice is not the employee's alone, as at any point the company may tell an individual that they will be made redundant. But during the emotional roller-coaster process, this point is when the employee begins the process of being a survivor – this is when they start to take actions to enhance those chances of being successful. Before this time, they may not have been psychologically ready to do so.

From this time, the outlook continues to improve (unless some unexpected external event or piece of information pushes one back a few steps, which can happen). Once the situation is accepted, it isn't a big step to becoming impatient because inevitably things start to move more slowly. Some people will eventually be excited about the new organization and ideally feel that they are actually much better off in the new company than their old one (assuming that the deal overall will be a success, which isn't assured, as noted earlier).

The above cycle of reactions and emotions is never smooth. The time of personal progression through these steps differs for every employee. As noted above, there can even be backward steps, and at any point the employee may be forced off the curve through involuntary redundancy or by choosing to jump off the roller coaster and exiting the company. There are also external factors that affect this personal transition, such as the way in which family and friends react. Employees may experience domestic repercussions when work-related anxieties spill over into family life, particularly if they concern the financial implications of an uncertain job future or the possibility of relocation.

The power of positive thinking

"When I came to Gillette I knew already about the acquisition [by Procter & Gamble]. There was some uncertainty, but there wasn't any anxiety or panic. On the contrary I was looking forward to new career perspectives and potential benefits."

Country head of IT, P&G

It isn't until the upswing in the above curve – the point when there's acceptance of the change brought about by the merger – that the organization begins once again to have productive employees with a positive approach. This then begins a virtuous circle that reinforces not only the emotions and work of those employees but of other survivors. It becomes more than just survival. Employees can use the situation of an M&A deal to grow personally and find greater opportunities within the new entity – rather than just surviving.

But until that point is reached, survival will become an obsession to the extent that trying to maintain personal status, prestige, and power becomes all-important and overrides organizational goals. Many people who leave the organization either through redundancy or choice will leave colleagues behind who may feel angry, resentful, or upset by their departure. With all these departures and the general chaos of the deal, the workload increases for those who remain.

Dealing with organizational change and self

"Any form of organizational change can threaten our sense of self, through undermining the structure of functional groupings, so that previously held beliefs about in-groups and out-groups, as sustained through gossip and story-telling, are no longer necessarily valid. In other words, the labels we use to define ourselves and others – our heroes and villains, leaders and fools – are called into question and hence the firm ground upon which we build our personal identity edifice begins to shake."

Alexandra Stubbings, specialist in organizational identity and culture change, Ashridge Consulting

---

Investors pressure management to achieve efficiencies and cost-cuts, and the synergies between the two companies are often the principal financial benefit from the deal. Thus, almost every

M&A transaction results in reductions in the workforce, as noted before. However, given that we live in a society where occupational achievements have become a measure for personal and professional recognition and fulfillment, losing your job following a merger has become more than an end to its monetary benefits. Not only are employees losing their jobs and thus the link to their work colleagues, they often also fall out (or fear falling out) of the social group they belong to. This helps explain why job loss through an M&A deal is so traumatic.

CHANGING PRODUCTIVITY

While employees may be experiencing the anxieties described above, they may be reluctant to expose any sign of vulnerability, or give any indication that they are not tough or fit enough for the post-merger organization. For many managers, voicing objections to post-acquisition changes and risking earning the label "resistant to change" is considered to be the kiss of death for their future career prospects; employees at all levels recognize that this is the time when they have to show they are worth retaining.

But despite these noble efforts to continue working as before or even with greater resolve, it is difficult to maintain this level of attention to the job when there is such concern and uncertainty about the future. Dennis Kozlowski, the Chairman and CEO of Tyco Industries, said in the *Harvard Business Review* in May 2000 that productivity for people declines during a merger from their normal 5.7 hours in an eight-hour work day to less than one hour.

Different people in the organization react differently, and at different rates depending on your level in the organization. As shown in Figure 4.3, the senior managers who know about the deal before it is announced will be gradually distracted by the deal early in the process as it gains momentum and certainty, and then when the intensity of the deal increases after the announcement

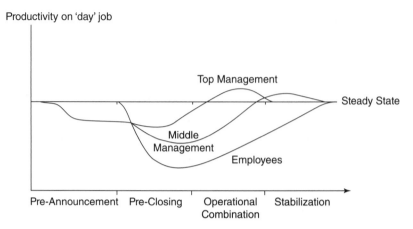

Figure 4.3   Productivity levels of different groups of employees

will be even more distracted. Ultimately, this group – or at least those who plan to remain with the company – will be excited about the deal and more productive than normal for the period after closing. Others in the firm won't be affected at all before the announcement because they are unaware of the deal, but their first reaction to the deal will be very quick and strong. Since they have less control over the transaction and their daily work, their productivity will be more affected as they try to figure out exactly what the acquisition or merger means for them. Middle managers, with somewhat more control over their jobs, should pull out of this sooner than lower level employees.

All levels of employee are affected. The 2002 CIPD redundancy practices survey suggested that 8% of those who were fired in that year were senior managers, 24% managers and professionals, another 24% skilled non-manual workers, and 20% were skilled manual workers. Although this survey wasn't specific to M&A deals and looked at all causes of redundancy, it is not unreasonable to assume that the figures would be similar following a merger or acquisition. Depending on level, individuals tend to react differently. By the time a deal is announced, senior executives are likely to be ready to complete and take on the task of integration at full speed but lower level employees who just learned about the deal still require more time and support to wrestle with their own fear and anxiety. It is often the case that senior managers stop communicating, are not empathetic, and do not manage their employees' feelings and problems, not for lack of interest in seeing the deal complete successfully, but because they don't understand that those other employees are at a different point psychologically in accepting the deal than they are.

Employees respond differently not only based on their level in the organization, but according to their division or location. When Procter & Gamble acquired Gillette in 2005, in Russia, it was reported that well over 50% of the Gillette employees left following the merger (not all immediately) which was a much higher attrition rate than the company globally. This may have been due to the company deciding that the Russian divisions needed significant restructuring, but it also may have been due to employees responding differently there than elsewhere in the company and voluntarily choosing not to remain with the newly combined company.

EFFECT ON THOSE REMAINING

The effect of redundancy is not restricted to those who have left, but extends to those remaining in the company as well. Those left in the organization might experience what is called "survivor syndrome." Originally describing the feelings that survivors of horrific events felt when others involved were permanently disabled or died, this term applies as well in a different sense to M&A deals. It refers in this instance to employees feeling guilty that their colleagues have been made redundant, but not them. The reactions of "survivors" can be very different, with some fearing that they will still lose their job at some point in the future, others feeling guilt that it was not they who were made redundant, and still others being concerned about the well-being of their ex-colleagues. Regardless of which reaction, it results in lower morale and decreasing commitment, trust, and loyalty towards the organization among the survivors. If companies try to deal with this "survivor syndrome" by demonstrating to the remaining employees that the process for determining redundancies was transparent and professional, and that those made redundant were treated fairly and lawfully, the general productivity and morale are less likely to be affected adversely.

Some employees simply will not be affected. They may have been lucky enough to work in a division with no overlap with the other company or in a geographical location where the other company didn't operate. This leads to three groupings of individuals: those who are not affected by the deal (although this situation could change suddenly), those affected by the deal but who are likely to stay and therefore not stressed by it because they see it as an opportunity to enhance their position (and these people too should be aware that their personal circumstances could also change rapidly), and those who are faced with certain or potential redundancy.

Very often it will be most difficult for employees who were previously competitors with their new colleagues: Exxon merging with Mobil, British Petroleum and Amoco, Hewlett Packard and Compaq, Glaxo Welcome and Smithkline Beecham, Price Waterhouse and Coopers & Lybrand, Bank of America and Merrill Lynch and the list goes on. In these companies, workers who had been vicious competitors now have to work together as a team. According to Alexandra Stubbings of Ashridge Consulting, "Mergers between competitors are particularly fraught with difficulty for members who are used to constructing the 'other' as the enemy. There is a strong tendency to homogenize the other and to attribute negative qualities to them. Any marginal or counter-cultural behavior that is attributable to one member becomes amplified and exaggerated such that it applies to all. One can start by changing the high-profile symbols – the signs on the doors and the letter-heads – but one cannot expect people to think differently about themselves overnight."

This process can take years. John Mack, CEO of Morgan Stanley, said in 2007 – eight years after his company merged with Dean Witter – that it was only then that some of the last changes were made to eliminate the final vestiges of the two separate prior companies (in that case, eliminating a duplicate broker dealer subsidiary that had retained the Dean Witter name for all those years after the merger).

Mergers and acquisitions have a tendency to bring out the worst in people. Managers and other employees *are* looking out for themselves first, as many of the people we spoke to who had been through deals told us. In fact, each of the Biblical seven deadly sins seems to rear its ugly head during these deals, as shown in Figure 4.4.

Some people may respond differently, and there is evidence that as more and more deals occur – and as more people have experienced a merger or know someone well who has – that they will learn better how to manage their responses to the announce-ment of a deal involving their company. A survey by Towers Perrin in 2004 claimed to disprove the generally accepted view that productivity declines during a merger or acquisition. On the

Greed:	Give me a better job with more money or give me a bigger redundancy package
Pride:	I can do the job better than my counterpart in the other company: it's mine or I've got to leave
Lust:	Why can't I have the job she just got?
Envy:	Everyone's getting a better position (or redundancy package) than I am with this merger
Sloth:	I don't have to worry. I'll wait until the deal closes
Gluttony:	I can work on the integration committee *and* still do my day job fully
Anger:	I hate mergers and the idiot executives who came up with this deal; everything was fine before!

Figure 4.4 The seven deadly sins of employees in M&A deals

contrary, the majority of respondents stated that productivity had increased (or stayed the same) while admitting that morale and engagement did decline. Perhaps the remaining employees in this past merger cycle were more concerned with keeping their jobs by showing good performance. Or perhaps the greater volume of deals has demonstrated to many that losing your job because your company was acquired is no longer a "black mark" on your CV. It is possible to triumph over the adversity of a merger or acquisition.

CHAPTER 5

WHY SOME PEOPLE WIN AND OTHERS LOSE

Some people are more likely to succeed in a merger or acquisition than others. The Chartered Institute of Personnel and Development redundancy practices survey mentioned in earlier chapters found that the main criteria used by employers for selecting people to be made redundant included:

- 68% – the employee's role within the organization (where the people retained remained in positions that were largely unchanged after the acquisition, whereas those made redundant were asked to leave because their jobs no longer existed)
- 62% – job performance (in situations where only one job remained, the employee with the highest previous job performance was retained)
- 52% – the employee's flexibility (whether they were willing to take a different position in the new organization)

Research shows there to be several further characteristics of those more likely to succeed. These are personal factors such as experience with prior acquisitions, level of position in the firm, tenure, job role (front or back office), personality type, and even your personal situation (such as whether you are single or married) or are company factors such as whether you are with the acquirer or target, if the deal is hostile or friendly, and your division's location.

No one – not even the CEO of the acquirer – is assured of being able to stay. But the chances for some employees are better than others. Is this fair? Of course not. But knowing that you are in a group that is less likely to be retained may demonstrate that you need to work harder to better your chances. But be careful of complacency as well: even if you can tick several of the boxes of those more likely to succeed, there is no certainty for anyone.

As noted in Chapter 1, the interviews and surveys conducted for this book didn't look at factors where it would be illegal in most countries to discriminate in favor or against a group of employees or any individual, such as sex, race, country of origin, age, sexual orientation, physical or mental disability, or religion. There certainly may be managers who illegally and certainly inappropriately choose the people they fire based on these factors. There are legal remedies (in addition to other remedies within companies) to deal with this. If you do feel that you are or may be discriminated against because of race, age, disability, or any other such factors, you should stand up for your rights both in terms of talking to your line manager (even if he or she is the one doing the discriminating), your human resources department, any available works council or trade union, or even outside legal counsel.

The factors that can affect your positioning in terms of being more or less likely to be selected for redundancy are reviewed below in the two categories noted above: those that are individual factors and those of the company within which you work (the company prior to the acquisition). Many of these factors are related and affect each other.

INDIVIDUAL FACTORS

There are seven factors about you – the employee – that will contribute to determining whether you may be made redundant when your company acquires, is bought by, or merges with another organization. First is whether you work in the front or back office. Other factors include your own recent job performance, your personal experience with previous acquisitions, your level in the organization, how long you've been with the company, your personal situation (how flexible you are in terms of moving), and your personality type. These are discussed below.

Job role (client facing or back office)

There is a greater likelihood of being retained if you have profitable clients. Companies merging or acquiring usually place great importance on keeping clients, and therefore on the employees who have the closest contact with those clients. This is especially important because the turmoil surrounding a merger is usually a signal to competitors that they have an opportunity to take clients away from merging firms which are possibly or even likely to be neglecting their clients while they are distracted by internal issues related to the merger.

Maintaining revenues and demonstrating bottom-line profits are also critical at this time when the CEO and CFO are telling and retelling analysts, journalists, and shareholders that the deal makes perfect business sense – complete with no losses to revenue and maybe even increased sales.

Importance of keeping clients

"When we make an acquisition, we never want to lose any customers. Therefore, staff with client contact have the highest level of job security. Get as close to the customers as possible, or be someone who is critical to the customers."

Michel Akkermans, Chairman and CEO, Clear2Pay

Thus, front office staff who have demonstrated revenue-generating abilities are unlikely to be made redundant, unless they are in a division which is not being retained by the company or there is someone in the other company who covers the same clients. In this situation, it is unlikely that both would be made redundant immediately; more common is for both employees to be retained and work out the appropriate client coverage, although ultimately one of the two individuals is likely to leave.

Spotlight: Banco Santander/Abbey National

Retaining all front office staff

On Monday, July 26, 2004, Banco Santander of Spain announced its acquisition of Abbey National Bank in the UK. Abbey had been struggling for several years, with significant losses in its core mortgage lending business and some unsuccessful expansions into wholesale banking. Santander had been an aggressive acquirer of banks on the Iberian Peninsula and in Latin America, but this was its first acquisition in the UK.

Santander announced that by 2007 it aimed to cut €450 million worth of inefficiencies, including the removal of over 4000 jobs.

Immediately upon the completion of the acquisition of Abbey in mid-November 2004, Francisco Gómez-Roldán, the Chief Financial Officer of Grupo Santander, started work as Abbey's new CEO. He announced that 2000 staff would be made redundant by March 2005, but that no sales staff would be in this group of redundancies. During the process of agreeing the headcount reduction, there was an announcement that customer-facing staff would be banned from moving to non-front office roles. Further, all ex-front office staff were written to personally and asked to move back into sales. The messages from the staff reductions and the initiatives to strengthen the sales function were that the front office was of paramount importance and that everyone else was at risk.

Regarding job roles, most companies will decide to keep permanent staff ahead of temporary or project staff. In many deals, temporary staff are informed immediately that their contracts will be terminated as soon as possible (depending on the terms of those contracts). Among the permanent staff, those who are working on projects are also at risk if their project is discontinued or if non-project staff can complete the work.

Project staff at risk of redundancy

"As an individual, your period of greatest weakness is when you are coming to the end of a particular project (however successful) and are not yet sufficiently stuck into a new project to be indispensable. Or, put another way, people will be more focused on what you are doing in the process than what you have just done."

Partner, financial services firm

Although overall there doesn't appear to be much research that has been done recently on whether you are more at risk if you are in manufacturing or service industries, you will certainly find yourself out of a job if you work at an industrial plant that is no longer needed. Synergies, as noted earlier, are often one of the important reasons behind a deal taking place: the two companies that are combining are able to achieve the promised cost savings through job cuts but also by closing redundant plants, saving not just the people costs but also the facilities and non-personnel manufacturing expenses of operating that plant. If you are a worker in a factory that is relatively inefficient because it is old or uses out-dated technology, you can almost be certain that one reason a more efficient competitor purchases your company is because they plan to shut the plant and move the manufacturing to one of their newer plants. Your job is then certain to go.

Spotlight: Oracle/PeopleSoft

Back office support of client products

During the 2004 hostile takeover of PeopleSoft by Oracle, when over 40% of all employees at PeopleSoft were targeted for redundancy, Oracle said that it intended to retain more than 90% of PeopleSoft staff in the areas that developed and supported PeopleSoft products. According to the San Francisco Chronicle, this "move was an attempt to assure PeopleSoft customers who Oracle wanted to keep but who were afraid that Oracle might immediately drop the PeopleSoft system."

Job performance

The second most important factor in determining whether you will be made redundant or not is whether you have recently been performing well in the firm. If your last performance review was poor or if you already are on probation because of poor performance, then you will naturally be at the bottom of any list of people to be retained in the company. Prior performance reviews – sometimes as many as those for the past three years – will be used by transition and integration teams to determine who to keep and which positions they should assume.

The inverse is unfortunately less likely to be true, even if good reviews are nevertheless helpful. A history of excellent performance reviews will certainly not by itself place you on any list to be laid off. In fact, it may place you above others whose performance has been less stellar. Yet there are many people who have received the highest reviews in their prior company who find themselves redundant in the new organization because the roles have been changed (see an example in the Foreword to this book) or there is someone from the other company whose performance is just as good and is selected due to some of the other factors below or they were better able to position themselves for selection.

Experience with prior acquisitions

> **Been there, done that**
>
> "Every deal adds experience and you can then see the potential issues further out."
>
> *Senior executive, financial services industry*

The research conducted for this book found that one of the best predictors of success is to have had previous experience with acquisitions. These individuals were more successful at retaining their jobs in the next acquisition, even if they were by that point with a different firm. At middle management levels, where overall success rates were around 60–70%, over 85% of those who had been through more than three M&A deals were survivors of the next deal. These employees were better able to diagnose the situation from prior experience.

Better next time

"Having experienced several M&A deals (on both sides), I would be much better prepared in future."

Manager, finance firm

But, of course, you can't plan for the next acquisition (unless perhaps you are the CEO) and often it is serendipity that you find yourself in a company that is about to be acquired. So what other situations affect whether you are more or less likely to be retained following an M&A deal?

Experience counts

"There is no substitute for experience of an M&A transaction to understand the processes, pressures and politics."

Head of mergers, acquisitions and disposals, manufacturing firm

---

Level of position

Many managers can deal with an acquisition better than their staff because they are closer to the decision-makers and the information flow. (Although do note that sometimes the exact opposite is true when lower level employees may be more in the information loop, as discussed in Chapter 8.) Managers, if they do have better information about a deal, can use that information inappropriately to their own personal advantage by withholding key facts from their team and others. This may, at least in the short term, provide them with an advantage in the zero-sum game of retaining a job.

At more senior levels in the organization, the chances of being retained in the same job decline dramatically. In most companies, there is room only for one CEO, one CFO, one chief technology officer, one head of marketing, etc. Thus, assuming one of the two incumbents from the two merging firms is not willing to take a demotion and report to the other, the chances of survival are only 50% – much lower than the average shown earlier in most deals where the overall chances of survival in a company are approximately 90%. Just below the executive suite, similar situations occur – with chances of survival greater than 50/50, but still less than the average.

Tougher at the top

"Since the companies were in essentially the same business, there was little need for additional management talent – particularly at the upper levels."

Partner, real estate investment firm

There's another reason why more senior employees will be at greater risk of redundancy than junior employees. Often in a merger, there is a cost reduction figure given to each department to achieve as part of the drive for efficiency in putting the two companies together. In order to achieve the cost reduction, fewer senior staff (who are paid more) need to be made redundant than the lower-paid junior staff. For example, when Banco Santander of Spain acquired Abbey National Bank in the UK, each department was given specific headcount *cost* targets, for example 13% in risk and 30% in IT (this deal was shown earlier in this chapter). This put senior staff at greater risk than their junior colleagues due to their relative expense, and consequently led to the removal of many of Abbey's old guard who had large salaries through long service to the company.

Tenure

According to a survey conducted in 2008 by Cass Business School graduate students Mark Dickenson and Gareth Wood for this book, there were differences in the likelihood of redundancy depending on how long an individual had been with a company (see Figure 5.1). The highest retention rate was those who had been with the company for less than one year (perhaps because many of these may still have had guaranteed contracts or been hired for a specific role or skill that remained), and also those who had been with the firm for between five and 10 years (where these individuals had been with the firm long enough to be expert in their areas but not so long that they are the most highly paid or in the senior management positions among which, as seen above, the redundancy rates are higher). Those least likely to be retained had been with their companies for only two to five years or, as can perhaps be expected, those over 10 years (despite the redundancy packages probably being larger for this last group).

This was in distinct contrast to the conventional wisdom that M&A redundancies follow the accountancy LIFO ("last in, first out") policy that "everyone who has been here for less than two years goes." In their survey, survival rates for employees with tenures less than that period were actually superior to the overall norm. These differences in success at staying are not great and perhaps the most important factor about tenure may be that it helps employees to spot opportunities ahead of the crowd. In a situation where every tiny advantage may be critical, this could have an effect on the ability to retain your job.

Tenure	Outcome	
	Stayed	Left
Less than 1 year	79%	21%
1–2 years	75%	25%
2–5 years	65%	35%
5–10 years	80%	20%
>10 years	67%	33%
Total sample	74%	26%

Figure 5.1   Influence of tenure on retention outcome
Source: Dickenson and Wood, Cass Business School (2008)

It appears that the reason that tenure is not a critical factor is because it can work both for and against an employee. A company undergoing a restructuring as dramatic as a merger or acquisition needs employees and managers who will be flexible within an organization that is likely to be changing for several years. People who have been with an organization for a long time will certainly bring experience (a positive) but may also be less flexible (a negative) than those less wedded to the ways and culture of the legacy company. Also, longer tenure is certainly correlated with higher income as longer-serving employees work their way up the organization. As seen above, those who are paid more and those who are in more senior positions are more likely to be made redundant than the average lower-paid junior employees.

Personal situation

It may not be legal or ethical to make decisions about who to hire on the basis of nationality, age, or family situation, but there are times when these factors have been taken into account in decisions about who to retain or fire. For example, there were three partners in a hedge fund in Australia which was bought by a UK-based investment bank; two of the partners were Australian, and both had families and large mortgages, while the third was single and originally from Ireland. The investment bank said they only wanted to retain two partners in Australia. Although they left the decision about who would stay to the three partners, it was quickly understood among the three that the Irishman would be the one to leave, which he did voluntarily, as he would be least affected by being out of a job and have the greatest flexibility in seeking a new job in another location. Flexibility in moving positions within a company is also important, as will be discussed in Chapter 10. This can often be as much a factor as having a diverse set of skills and experience, and a willingness to use these in another job within the newly combined company.

Age-related decisions are often communicated in terms of "experience" or "skills." Family situation can often be handled similarly, as single people tend to be younger than those with larger families. There's no way to tell if these factors ever do come into play, but some managers will privately say that they do take them into account "all other factors being equal."

Personality type

The results from one of the surveys conducted for this book found that there is a rough correlation between personality types and their behavior in an M&A situation. Beyond mere survival, some people with certain personality types were able actually to exploit the situation. These were employees who managed not just to "make the best of a bad situation," but to better their position through careful exploitation of the confusion that reigned around them in the midst of the corporate changes. In fact, there were some individuals who apparently had the experience and confidence to seek out such situations, believing that they could advance up the corporate ladder more quickly through being part of multiple M&A deals.

Those most likely to survive tended to be extroverted, conscientious, and emotionally stable. Not surprisingly, those individuals who were open to new experiences tended to exploit the deal; they were equally likely to do that by staying at the firm or even by leaving the company for an improved role elsewhere, but having emphasized the merger experience gained (even if only for a short while) in the M&A deal.

Individuals who were consummate team players and those who tended to avoid confrontation were least likely to exploit the M&A process due to the fact that they were more likely to prioritize general affability over personal competitiveness. They also tended to be more likely to be made redundant. M&A deals are not for the shy or friendly, it seems. An element of self-preservation and selfishness seems to go a long way toward enhancing your ability to be a survivor in a firm that is combining with another.

Politics, as will be discussed in greater detail in Chapter 11, will also play an important role; many survivors said that those who were willing to play the political game were more likely to be retained. Clearly, these survivors were also opportunistic: they seized upon the instability of the M&A situation to engage in political maneuvering for personal benefit.

Necessity for politics

"It's impossible to not play politics (just saying you won't is a political statement!) but one can attempt to hold a position without antagonizing; not easy, but attempting to really listen, really inquire into the other's perspective without judgment is a good place to start."

Alexandra Stubbings, specialist in organizational identity
and culture change, Ashridge Consulting

COMPANY FACTORS

There are also some critical factors about the company which determine whether you are more or less likely to be made redundant when your company combines with another. These include whether the company is the acquirer or target (or whether it is a merger of equals), whether the deal is hostile or friendly, and your office's location.

Target or acquirer

The Dickenson/Wood survey in 2008 also looked at differences in departures (whether voluntary or involuntary) between targets and acquirers. In this case, conventional wisdom was correct that employees in acquiring companies were more likely to stay: 88% of those in acquiring companies remained in their jobs whereas only 64% did in the target company. This means that over one-third of target company employees will be asked or decide to leave following an acquisition. This has significant implications for companies acquiring other firms and clearly this needs to be taken into account when planning for the post-acquisition period or even whether to proceed with the deal in the first place. It also demonstrates the very significant impact of being acquired on the employees of the target, both those who are made redundant and those who remain whose friends and colleagues have now gone.

> **Advantage acquirer**
>
> "Essentially, one of the reasons for the merger was to increase efficiencies of scale – hence some positions were inevitably redundant. The only question is who has the best talent to fill them. The acquirer found it easier to keep the existing people in place, rather than take a chance on new and unknown people – particularly if they appeared negative and unco-operative."
>
> *Partner, real estate investment firm*

If the target is acquired because the bidder knew that they had a weakness, then it might be better to be in the target than the acquirer in the particular units sought by the purchaser. Thus, for example, when Deutsche Bank, at that time Europe's largest bank, acquired the 8th largest bank in the USA (Bankers Trust) in 1999, Deutsche was looking for greater strength in investment banking and a larger US presence. Thus, it is no surprise that the newly appointed co-heads of Investment Banking at Deutsche Bank following the acquisition both came from Bankers Trust and that the former head of Investment Banking from Deutsche Bank departed. Little more than a decade earlier, Deutsche Bank had acquired Morgan Grenfell in the UK, and, as shown in the story below, again there were people from Deutsche Bank who "lost" in the battle to remain in key positions at the bank.

Spotlight: Deutsche Bank/Morgan Grenfell

Advantage target

"Deutsche Bank bought Morgan Grenfell in 1989 but only in 1995 did the operations actually merge. At this time, I was a project manager at the London branch of Deutsche Bank and still relatively junior. Significant parts of Deutsche Bank London at this time, including the function I belonged to, were driven by German expatriates.

"Deutsche's management hoped that the merger of Deutsche and Morgan Grenfell in London would transform the commercial bank into an investment bank. Therefore, it was not surprising that the senior managers of Morgan Grenfell, the larger operation in London, were dominating the merger activities supported by the German board members. My mentor at this time was a senior German

> manager who was losing out in the London merger battle – and was therefore offered a senior position back in Germany which he accepted.
>
> "For me things also changed: I lost not only my mentor, but the in-house project management team we had in Deutsche London was not a concept known in Morgan Grenfell. Therefore, the department was dismantled. Luckily, I found an 'interim'-management position in Operations to take my chances in the newly-created Deutsche Morgan Grenfell."
>
> *Currently senior director,*
> *asset management company*

Hostile or friendly deal

Despite some notable exceptions, as shown above, it is usually a disadvantage to be in the target company. This is even truer in a hostile takeover where the likelihood of retaining a job in the target is even lower than in friendly deals where there is usually a greater attempt on the part of the acquirer to make sure that people from the target obtain jobs in the new organization.

In a hostile deal, there is no pretense of who is taking over whom. There is usually little that has been done before the deal closes to build a common culture and to foster the professional relationships between the two companies that would help target employees to be retained. In fact, in deals where the hostility has been particularly intense, the buyer will be explicit in announcing that senior executives and perhaps other layers of management will be fired upon completion of the deal because of their intransigence if not outright hostility during the purchase negotiations.

In a hostile takeover, it is usually more explicit as well that the acquiring company intends to change the target. There may be fewer attempts to incorporate the culture, systems, and employees of the target. The acquired company's employees will need to adapt to the new organization or leave, and many will be uncomfortable with the abrupt change or unwilling to modify their way of doing business.

Hostile takeovers

"My experience was of a hostile takeover. I was on good terms with the old management but I had to quickly build relationships with key new management. It worked, but I left because I didn't share the same values as them. The culture had changed; they were more aggressive and threatening. I'm self-sufficient and independent and I don't react kindly to unfounded threats. So I left. I wasn't bitter or anything and I'm still on good terms with them, but I never told them the real reasons for leaving."

Sales manager, retail firm

Location

Different countries have different attitudes towards redundancy and different statutory requirements (as discussed in Chapter 3), but other issues related to where your office is located will affect whether you are likely to be made redundant.

There will be different cultural aspects to the handling of redundancy depending on where you work. Especially for the remaining employees and the ability in the future to attract new employees, these issues can sometimes be more important to understand than the legal requirements. There are two types of cultural issues: external (for example, relating to the specific industry or the country in which the company operates) and internal (related to the company itself, but which may also differ according to division or country). The importance of understanding the nature of relationships between employees at all levels and the

social factors of corporate culture will play a major role in understanding the way in which redundancy can be made smoother
with the fewest knock-on effects for those who remain with the
organization. Although many large companies ignore these differences and apply the same redundancy policies to all or most of
their branches globally, there are other companies which will
properly reflect these local differences in their redundancy policies.
This then affects whether one would be more or less likely to be
made redundant, if located in a particular country.

For example, one would be less likely to be made redundant
where legal requirements for redundancy are stricter and make the
cost of a redundant employee higher or the process longer (e.g.
many countries in continental Europe), or where the culture per-
ceives redundancy severely (e.g. Japan).

Another aspect about location is whether there are cost (especially salary and wage) differences between the locations of the
target and acquirer. If one is located in lower cost areas, it is more
likely that staff will be retained in those locations. Often, acquiring
a company with a lower employee cost profile is one of the principal drivers to acquisition, so if it is the case that the target's costs
are lower, then the acquiring company's staff may be at greater risk
of redundancy – a reverse of what would be expected. A related
point is whether the acquirer or target is located in an area considered to be more attractive based on other factors – schooling,
housing, general economic conditions, state or local government
financial support, or any other reason. If you are working in such
an area, you do have an advantage over employees from the other
company in a less attractive location.

Lastly, target company employees are more likely to be retained
when the acquisition is made principally for geographic expansion
reasons. One Eastern European manager and veteran of several
acquisitions in the telecommunications industry said that he always
survived because when his companies were purchased, it was
always to add to the geographic scope of the acquirer: the buyers

rarely had any presence in Eastern Europe and when they did, it was a much smaller branch operation than his. Therefore, he and his team were always the experts in the region. They were kept employed, often with large retention packages to make sure they wouldn't leave.

ASSESSMENT OF YOUR OWN VULNERABILITY

It is useful to look at all of these factors to see whether you are more or less likely to be made redundant when you hear that your company is or might be combining with another company. Tick a box in each row in Figure 5.2 and then add up the number of ticks in each column. If a row does not relate to you or your company, then leave it blank. The comparison of the relative number of boxes ticked in each column should indicate whether you are more likely to be asked to leave the company once it has merged, been acquired, or acquires another firm. For example, if you ticked four boxes in the "more likely" column, three in the "moderately likely," and two in the "less likely" columns, then you should conclude that you have a very good possibility of being one of the 10% or so of total staff to be made redundant, but certainly less of a chance than someone who would have ticked, say, five or six boxes in the "more likely" column. If you have a fairly even distribution across the columns or if you have similar numbers in both the "more likely" and "less likely" columns, then you are likely to be only at moderate risk of redundancy.

Naturally, this situation can change (a friendly deal can turn hostile, for example). Also, different companies and even different managers will place different weight on the various factors, so you will need to assess whether one or more should receive greater emphasis. For example, if the company has announced that it is

	More likely to be made redundant		Moderately likely		Less likely to be made redundant	
Individual factors	Back office job (e.g. HR, IT, payroll)	☐	Back office directly supporting sales (e.g. product development, R&D, product control)	☐	Sales and other front office	☐
	Poor performance review recently	☐	Average performance review recently	☐	Excellent performance review recently	☐
	No experience with acquisitions previously	☐	Some experience with acquisitions	☐	Extensive experience previously with acquisitions	☐
	Senior executive	☐	Manager	☐	Staff	☐
	2 to 5 years' tenure with the company, or over 10 years	☐	1–2 years	☐	Less than 1 year with the company or between 5 and 10 years	☐
	Inflexible to move, large mortgage or other debts, many dependents	☐	Moderate flexibility to move, moderate mortgage, few dependents	☐	Flexible to move, no mortgage, no dependents	☐
	Team player and conflict avoider	☐	Neither	☐	Personality is extroverted, conscientious, stable, willing to play politics	☐
Company factors	Target company employee	☐	Neither, the deal is a merger of equals	☐	Working in the acquirer	☐
	Hostile deal (and positioned in target)	☐	Neither friendly nor hostile deal	☐	Friendly deal (positioned in either company) or hostile (and working in the acquirer)	☐
	Easy to make employees redundant (government regulations and cultural norm)	☐	Moderate	☐	Difficult	☐
	Currently working in relatively unattractive local markets (high wages, supplier costs, and taxes)	☐	Moderately attractive local markets	☐	Attractive local markets from the company's perspective	☐
	Totals for each column					
	More likely to be made redundant		Moderately likely		Less likely to be made redundant	

Figure 5.2 Reality check: likelihood of being made redundant during an acquisition

making the acquisition to reduce expenses in the back office (as Banco Santander did with its acquisition of Abbey National as shown in the Spotlight case study earlier in this chapter), then this factor should be emphasized more and maybe you should put two or more ticks in the relevant box on that row.

WHO IS MORE LIKELY TO SURVIVE?

Of course, the reason you are retained may just be plain luck. Someone may be retiring at exactly (or near) the time of the merger. For example, this made the decision of which CEO to keep easier in the merger between The Bank of New York and Mellon mentioned in Chapter 3. If you're lucky, your counterpart at the other company may leave quickly for a competitor after the deal announcement.

It's better to be lucky ...

"One lesson is that you really have no idea what is really going on in the bidder until after the deal proceeds. I didn't know that the head of my department at the buyer was so hated by everyone in the company that they were looking for someone else – anyone else! – to take his place. I was lucky."

Head of legal, European bank

There are exceptions to every rule in M&A. In fact, one can truly say that no two deals are alike. Thus, there are no silver bullets about who will succeed in retaining their job. No guarantees. If the CEO of the larger company buying a smaller one can't be certain he or she will have a job once the dust has settled, then anyone else must be at risk of redundancy as well. Not that certain circumstances don't give you an edge: ideally, therefore, one would want to be a single, extrovert, somewhat selfish front office salesperson with loyal clients in the acquiring firm located in a country (say, in Scandinavia, Germany, or France) where it is difficult to make employees redundant and where the target doesn't operate. But even such people will occasionally be fired when their company has done a deal.

Thus, you need to move beyond the situation in which you find yourself – the factors noted above – to take some proactive steps in order to enhance your chances of being retained.

CHAPTER 6

THE M&A PROFESSIONALS

For most employees, M&A is a traumatic experience that may occur a few times over the course of a long career. For some people, however, M&A is a way of life. These are the professionals – the investment bankers, lawyers, accountants, and consultants – who make the M&A world go round. They work very hard with and for the managements of merging companies to make the deals happen. Most employees will never see these advisors, but they are critical to the deal process.

For the advisors, survival isn't the need to retain a job when a deal is announced. In fact, with each deal their personal marketability increases. The stresses for these advisors are in the type of work they do and how they do it: deal after deal, often jumping from one transaction to the next with very little, if any, break. This chapter shows what these people do, and how it affects you, as an employee.

Because most advisors want to see the deal complete, their motivations and goals are in direct conflict with most employees: while completion equals success for the advisors, most of the time it means redundancy to a large group of staff of the two companies that are combining. As we have seen in the previous chapters, there are few employees who can be absolutely certain their job will be secure after the deal closes. Most employees caught up in a deal will not have direct contact with these advisors, but many do as we will outline below.

Although there are often many advisors, this chapter will largely focus on the two largest groups: the investment bankers and the lawyers. Amy Howlett and Simon Solomon of Cass Business School spent time interviewing a cross-section to try to understand their activities better. This has been supplemented by the author's own experience in the industry over more than two decades and numerous conversations with many M&A practitioners that he has had in the past two years for this book.

WHO ARE THEY?

Financial advisors are usually from the investment banks brought in to provide technical, market, industry, and financial skills to support the selection, pricing, financing, structuring, negotiation, and closing stages of the deal. They often support the acquirer by providing financing for the deal as well, in purchasing shares of the target and providing loans to the company if required. Very often the investment bank will coordinate the other advisors on behalf of management, although in smaller deals the law or accounting firm will do this. They share the risk involved with the acquisition process in that the success of the deal can often influence their reputation and fees. Success for the investment banker means that the deal reaches closing (if representing a buyer or seller who wants the deal to take place) or is prevented from taking place (in the relatively rare cases when the investment bank is representing a target that is resisting a hostile bid). They typically are not involved in the deal after closing, unless their firm (and usually a different division) has provided financing, in which case they are focused at that point on making sure that the company is efficiently run with enough cash to pay the interest on any debt used to finance it. "Efficiently run" normally means the newly combined firm needs to do the same or even more with less, and this usually results in headcount reductions, as we have seen.

Investment bankers (see Figure 6.1 for job roles) need not sit in a pure investment bank and there are anyway fewer of these than several years ago due to consolidations in the industry, as with the acquisition in 2008 of Merrill Lynch by Bank of America, a number of high profile bankruptcies including the famous demise of Lehman Brothers in the same year, and the transformation of the two leading investment banks, Goldman Sachs and Morgan Stanley, into more traditionally regulated banks in the USA soon thereafter. Investment bankers can work in one of the remaining pure investment banks (typically called "merger boutiques") or another bank of various sorts that will have an investment banking division. However, most of the M&A advice given by investment bankers on the large deals that make headlines will be provided by a small group of companies known as the "bulge bracket" firms. Although the membership of this elite group changes, typically the list of bulge bracket firms will include Goldman Sachs, Morgan Stanley, Bank of America (with Merrill Lynch), J.P. Morgan, Citibank, Deutsche Bank, UBS, and Credit Suisse.

Legal advisors work in the law firms who advise and counsel organizations involved in the acquisition process, providing technical legal skills critical to the negotiation and closure of the deal (see Figure 6.2 for a list of the typical job roles in law firms). They draft agreements, coordinate all of the legal documents (of which there are many), conduct legal due diligence, and provide the principal regulatory advice. They are particularly visible in

Job titles	Age range	Typical responsibilities
• Analyst • Researcher	21–26	General support when pitching for new business and in executing deals: gathers secondary data; develops and updates financial models; produces presentations, may contact junior members at clients but generally represents the support "behind the scenes"
• Associate • Senior associate • Assistant vice-president	24–32	Coordinates the daily work in executing a deal; contact with clients on a day-to-day basis although not at a senior level; writes presentations and occasionally delivers parts; expected to develop a focused expertise in products and markets and will increasingly specialize
• Vice-president	26–35	Manages overall quality control of new business pitches and deal presentations; manages deal teams; is recognized client, product, or market expert; relationship manager for established clients
• Senior vice-president • Executive director (ED) • Principal	30–45 (and sometimes to retirement)	Builds and maintains client relationships at the highest (usually board) level; heads small departments; develops new products or businesses; is recognized externally as an expert in a specialist area; identifies the key internal team leaders for particular assignments
• Partner • Managing director (MD) • Executive vice-president	35–retirement	Helps determine the strategic direction of the investment banking division; leads business development in entire industry sectors/client groups; helps build and maintain relationships with large clients and other external bodies (regulators, government officials, etc.); coordinates activities across geographic boundaries within the group

Note that the specific titles and responsibilities will differ by company and the age ranges shown are approximations only, as there will be high performing individuals who will be promoted faster and younger; those not promoted to the next level by the upper age level shown will typically leave the company if not even the industry.

Figure 6.1 Job roles in investment banking (M&A departments)

hostile deals, as the legal challenges to the takeover often form an important part of the target company's defense. In comparison to financial advisors, legal firms share less risk with the client because their fees are not as dependent on the success of the transaction completing, although, as with investment banks, their reputation is. Unlike the investment bankers, their work often continues well

Job title	Age range	Typical responsibilities
Trainee	21–24	Rotates among different practice areas; supports associates in conducting research and producing documents
Junior associate	22–26	Researches precedents; assists with drafting a variety of documents; conducts due diligence research; often responsible for production of documents; supports more senior associates in executing deals
Mid-level associate	24–32	Manages day-to-day execution of a deal; acts as main contact with client staff at a junior level; drafts documents; develops internally recognized expertise in a specific legal and regulatory area; negotiates some of the terms in the legal agreements
Senior associate	26–35	Leads and manages overall quality of deals including structuring aspects; provides product or marketing expertise; acts as principal contact with clients; supports and attends marketing pitches
Junior partner	35–retirement	Leads and builds client relationships; project manages large or challenging deals; ultimate responsibility for quality and profitability; coaches and develops associates; heads internal groups or departments; develops new products or businesses; determines internal administrative policies; acts as an ambassador for the firm, networking with regulators, investment bankers, and others externally
Senior partner	40–retirement (very rare for partners to be working past 55)	

Note that the specific titles and responsibilities will differ by company and the age ranges shown are approximations only, as there will be high performing individuals who will be promoted faster and younger; those not promoted to the next level by the upper age level shown will typically leave the company if not even the industry.

Figure 6.2 Job roles in law firms (M&A departments)

past closing and into the integration period; some of this work is related to the new employment contracts for those people remaining with the newly combined company or the redundancy packages for the leavers.

Most of the leading law firms today would defy characterization as being regional or from a single country or city, but the largest law firms have traditionally been known in London as the "Magic Circle" (Allen & Overy, Clifford Chance, Freshfields Bruckhaus Deringer, Linklaters, and Slaughter and May); the similar group of US-headquartered law firms includes Cleary Gottlieb, Cravath Swaine, Simpson Thacher, Skadden Arps, Sullivan & Cromwell, and Wachtell Lipton.

Of the other advisors, the accountants are the next largest group although in some deals the sheer number of professionals working on the deal from the accounting firms may exceed the number of lawyers or investment bankers. These accountants conduct the lion's share of the due diligence which means that they need to have access throughout the two companies (and principally within the target company) to identify any potential problems with the deal and clarify for the buyer exactly what they are buying. This may start before the deal is announced but will grow in intensity once it is public. Few areas of the target will avoid having some analysis conducted on what they do, and in some cases this will extend to the bidder as the post-merger integration strategy is being determined, including how many employees will be required in the company after closing. The accountants also will be working with management in preparing financial projections and may also provide an independent valuation of the price being paid for the target. In some cases, principally medium-sized and small deals, the accounting firms will act as the investment bankers. There are also large teams in these large accounting firms that will work with management on the post-merger integration, often for many years.

Globally, the largest accounting firms are known as "The Big Four" which is composed of Deloitte Touche Tohmatsu, Ernst & Young, KPMG, and PricewaterhouseCoopers. Interestingly, the concentration of power in these four firms was the result of mergers that took place in the late 1980s and 1990s between what were then known as "The Big Eight," so the survivors from that period in these accounting firms have first-hand knowledge of what transpires in a merger.

Other consultants will be engaged by the two companies before and after announcement, and in the newly combined company after closing. These will include human resources consultants who will provide advice on the required staffing levels, terms of employment, and redundancy procedures. Especially important in hostile deals but present in most mergers and acquisitions will be the consultants who advise on public relations, investor relations (for communications with the owners of the two companies, which in many cases will be a diverse group of shareholders), and internal communications with staff.

HOW THEY WORK

By reputation, M&A advisors are hard-working, high-earning professionals. For example, excessive hours are compensated in the investment banks by very large bonuses, although in periods of lower deal volumes (such as occurred in 2008 and 2009), these bonuses may be a fraction of what they would be when the M&A wave peaks. The lawyers, accountants, and consultants are also well compensated, albeit not at the levels of the investment bankers and also without the extraordinarily large bonuses in the good years. These individuals put the company first with what seems like little regard to work/life balance issues. They are fiercely proud of their work and "wear their job on their sleeve" as one investment banker told us.

For the investment bankers and lawyers working on these deals, the 40-hour workweek is outdated. A 60-hour workweek would be considered by many in the field as being short enough to no longer brag about and is now considered practically part-time by some. Holidays and time with family and friends are rare, and the mere fact that one takes a holiday is frowned upon by some colleagues in this industry. Another reason is just that the business has a culture where work comes first no matter what time of the day or night and that the best quality product must be produced for the client no matter what the personal effort.

Perfection expected

"It's not one error in ten pages, it's zero errors."

Managing director, bulge bracket investment bank

Despite these apparent sacrifices for the firm and in working on each deal, these investment bankers and M&A lawyers love their jobs. In 2006, two surveys conducted by the Center for Work-Life Policy in the USA showed that, contrary to the expectation that these types of workers would be burned-out and bitter professionals, the majority of respondents (66% in the US sample, 76% in the global survey) loved their jobs. Almost two-thirds conceded that the intense nature of their work was a choice and more a function of the type of people they were.

Increasingly, the nature of M&A advisory business is global. These advisory firms work on a global basis and the individuals, no matter in which office they work, are expected to support their clients wherever they may be in the world. There have always been cross-border deals (companies buying or merging with foreign companies), but there have been many more of these deals since the early 1990s. Thus it is that a deal may involve a German or British company buying or merging with an American one (such as Daimler Benz, the parent of Mercedes, purchasing Chrysler or British Petroleum purchasing Amoco), an Indian company purchasing a British one (as with Tata buying Jaguar), or even a consortium of companies from various countries buying a firm in yet another country and splitting it up (as happened in 2007 to the Dutch bank ABN AMRO when it was purchased by a combination of the Royal Bank of Scotland based in the UK, Fortis of Belgium, and Banco Santander of Spain).

FOCUS ON THE DEAL

That same survey conducted by the Center for Work-Life Policy showed that, on average, 86% of high earners across various professions in the USA cited the stimulation, challenge, and adrenaline rush they get from their jobs as the main reason why they work as they do. Other motivators included high quality colleagues, high levels of compensation, recognition for work, and power and status. This is what is driving these individuals in the deal that is affecting your company. Whereas the company represents a lot more than just a place to collect a paycheck for most employees, to the deal advisors, the acquisition or merger is a financial, legal, or business transaction – just another in a series of deals that they are working on.

Adrenaline high

"There is something addictive about transaction work ... The adrenaline of a deal. There is a process where both parties want the deal to happen and it is exciting being part of that process."

Associate, New York-based law firm

This means that getting the deal done is important and these individuals will work very, very hard to make sure that the transaction does complete. As a firm, each has the accumulated experience in many cases of successfully completing thousands of deals, and any one partner or senior executive in charge of a particular deal may have worked on tens if not even hundreds of deals. They support the merging companies' management in making it happen, but need the rest of the organization to pull with them to make it a success. They have seen where previous deals have failed and what makes a deal succeed. By the time the deal is announced, there is momentum driving it to closing and making it difficult to derail unless something truly remarkable does happen to scupper the deal. In fact, approximately 70% of announced deals do complete. It is one of the principal responsibilities of these advisors to make sure this happens – uncovering any potential "showstoppers" and creatively finding solutions.

INTERACTION WITH THE DEAL ADVISORS

Whereas most employees in a company first find out about a deal only when it is announced, the advisors may have been working on it for a year or more. In some cases, they were the ones who proposed the deal to the CEO. In these cases, the advisors – usually the investment bankers – will have analyzed the market and identified companies where the merger or acquisition potential is high. When the time is right (and this may not happen immediately), they will approach the target's management to determine if they are willing to sell the whole company or even just a division if the acquisition would be for only part of the organization. Or they will approach the potential purchaser to determine if that buyer wishes to engage the investment bank to approach one or more targets and set the wheels in motion for an eventual acquisition.

Proud of the hard work

"… [I am] proud of this experience [closing a major deal] as it represented years of work with the one client. Success of a long-term relationship that was kept secret right until the end. [I] can still remember the Sunday when the deal was signed, especially the buzz and adrenaline."

M&A partner, law firm

A small number of people in the companies that are merging or being acquired will come into contact with these advisors before the deal is announced. These are typically the "insiders" to the deal and at the very highest levels of the organization. The pre-announcement group is kept small because of the risk of information leaking that a deal is pending. Research conducted at Cass Business School in 2008 sponsored by Intralinks showed that leaked deals were less likely to be completed and, if they did, would take longer. These deals are also more likely to attract other bidders, so that there's a risk that a competitor would walk away with the prize.

After the deal is announced, the advisors may be all over the company – conducting what is called "due diligence" when each company is trying to determine whether what it believed about the other company is true or not. The accountants, as noted above, but also investment bankers and lawyers will be involved with this process. There will also be human resources advisors, as discussed in Chapter 3, who will be assisting management with identifying which employees to retain and which post-closing positions they will occupy.

A DAY IN THE LIFE OF AN INVESTMENT BANKER

As noted earlier, this is a profession where 10–12 hour working days are considered the norm, and as the end of a deal approaches, this would extend to working through the night ("all-nighters"). For many employees within the company who do work with these advisors, this can be a very challenging change from their normal "business-as-usual" workday, although for some it can be an exciting time as well, especially if there's the possibility that having worked on the deal they may be more likely to be retained (and more on this in Chapter 12).

> **Long hours required**
>
> "Typically working weeks are either feast or famine. When no deal is on, the normal working day usually starts at 8:30 am and finishes about 7:00 pm. And when on a deal, the day starts at 8:30 am and can finish anywhere between 10 pm and midnight or even later. All-nighters occasionally, especially in the lead up to signing. It can also involve some weekend work."
>
> *M&A corporate lawyer and partner, law firm*

There's no such thing as a typical day in the life of an investment banker. Every day is different. To give an example, however, Figure 6.3 shows how a day for an associate working at a mid-sized investment bank in New York City or London might look during a period when working on an active deal. Few breaks, lots of stress, but knowledge that the work will be completed on time and with high quality.

ADVISORS ALSO NEED TO SURVIVE

There is no shortage of advisors for companies planning to merge with or acquire another company. Companies contemplating an M&A deal have their pick from a large number of advisors, although as in any industry, there's a first tier in greatest demand (as noted earlier in this chapter), second tier, and so on. It is a stressful environment for these advisors and thus parallels in many ways the stresses that executives, managers, and employees feel in their lives when their companies merge or acquire. The fact that mergers and acquisitions are now an accepted part of the general business environment doesn't make this any easier on those affected. There remains a need to focus on survival for everyone involved in these deals.

Time	Activity
5.00 am	Went to sleep.
6.00 am	Sleep.
7.00 am	Sleep.
8.00 am	Getting ready to go to work, checking emails on my BlackBerry and responding to urgent matters.
9.00 am	Read *The Wall Street Journal* on the way into work. Arrive at work. Check emails and respond to those that need my attention. Grab some breakfast to eat at my desk and catch up on news while eating quickly.
10.00 am	Continue working on my PC on the financial model that needs to be prepared for the Information Memorandum [a document for the client that details the pending deal process and financing].
11.00 am	While working on the model, start gathering material needed for a 1 pm call with the client. Finalize all the supporting documents and set up the conference call.
Noon	Order in lunch and continue working on the model. Colleagues ask for my help on their other parts of the Information Memorandum and I don't get to eat my lunch while it is warm.
1.00 pm	Participate on the call discussing the potential buyers of the company we are advising. I am being asked to summarize our model assumptions and walk the client's management through our analysis.
2.00 pm	The call is going on for longer than I anticipated. I am taking notes of tasks that need to be completed immediately after the call. When it ends, I discuss the assignment with my colleagues.
3.00 pm	Quickly eating (now cold) lunch and reading about my home football team. Have to focus again and continue working on the Information Memorandum. The senior bankers in the group requested a turn later this afternoon.
4.00 pm	While working on the industry section of the Information Memorandum, potential bidders call to ask questions about the opportunity and I walk them through the investment highlights.
5.00 pm	I try to get more of my financial model done and check in with my colleagues to see whether they completed the other tasks the vice-president asked for. I review the results and pass the analysis to my managing director. We get on the phone with the client's management and communicate the results (the managing director does all the talking).
6.00 pm	Back to the model. Senior bankers in our firm have asked to include a more detailed breakdown of the historical financial statements and I have to go back and start gathering more data. I contact the company and request more information so that I can complete this.
7.00 pm	I completed the valuation section and leveraged buyout analysis of the model and pass it on to my vice-president for his review. In the meantime, I check with my colleagues on their progress with the Information Memorandum and whether we have received a mark-up [reviewed copy with changes shown] yet.
8.00 pm	We order food and catch up on the news of the day. Still no mark-up. Waiting.
9.00 pm	I know we have to turn in the printed document tomorrow morning, so even though I am waiting for the mark-up to come back, I start working on the formatting so that we can cover as much ground as quickly as possible later in the night.
10.00 pm	We receive one mark-up via email, one through the fax machine, and a third one is handed to us from our MD as he leaves the office. It will be another late night. We divide up the work and try to go through the mark-ups.
11.00 pm	We double-check each other's work and make sure all the comments have been incorporated. We call the MD at his home to check what we should use when two mark-ups disagree with each other. The additional analysis, charts, and tables that have been requested take longer than anticipated.
Midnight	Still working to get the comments into the draft, we need some additional information from the company in the morning and leave placeholders in the book to indicate where these will go.
3.00 am	The analyst walks in with the revised turn of the Information Memorandum at 3 am. We proof it.
4.00 am	Travel home by taxi. Fall asleep in cab.
5.00 am	Go to sleep.

Figure 6.3 A day in the life of an M&A associate

The irony is that, especially with the economic, stock market, and M&A market declines that started in 2007 and hit banking and investment banking particularly hard, these investment banking firms are also merging, being acquired, or even going bankrupt … and thus these investment bankers will need to learn to survive when their own firms merge as well.

PART II

SURVIVING

CHAPTER 7

SHOULD I STAY OR SHOULD I GO?

Maybe you shouldn't want to stay with your company after it merges. You may have a better opportunity elsewhere, and a merger can be the trigger to move. Or this may be a good time to retire – and the company may even help you with a "sweetened" early retirement package. Even if you decide to stay, you may find that the company isn't what it was or what you expected it to be.

It could be the best thing that ever happened

"It could be a good opportunity to move on. It might just be the best thing to ever happen to you. A merger forces people to think out of the box. Forces people to rethink priorities, especially if you have a family."

Deputy chairman, New York-based bank

It's not just the victims of redundancy who suffer from a merger or acquisition, it's also the survivors. In the general population, Investors in People research on a UK sample of 2931 companies in late 2007 on the state of the UK workforce found that:

- 30% of UK employees are demotivated at work
- 43% are considering taking action and leaving their job in the next 12 months, with those that have been in their job for one to two years most likely to want to do so (48%)

It's likely to be even worse in firms that have recently merged.

Therefore, maybe you don't want to fight for your job once it's announced that there will be an acquisition. In most deals, motivation, job satisfaction, productivity, loyalty, and morale are lower even in those who remain with the company. This relates to the "survivor syndrome" mentioned in Chapter 4 and, as discussed there, also results from a breach of the psychological contract that every employee has with their employer. This is especially true in middle management layers where jobs and career opportunities change most after a merger or acquisition.

Disenchantment with the new company

"I have always been on the receiving end of a takeover. Cultural change is the biggest problem as you are now in a company that you didn't choose to be employed by. Have no loyalty to any company, look after yourself. If the new regime doesn't suit, then move on. You will be discarded very easily if it is found that you do not fit into the new organization."

Sales employee, telecoms firm

Research has also shown that managers and employees become more risk averse in their decision making post-acquisition. From this, one can imagine that surviving managers are less willing to "stick their neck out" following the redundancies that are inherent in all mergers and acquisitions. Management can even become panic stricken, as discussed below, and counterproductive.

DECISIONS, DECISIONS, DECISIONS ...

Whether to stay or leave may be a simple question, but to make an informed answer, you must consider a number of factors:

- First, whether you are confident in your ability to land a position in the new company when there may be a very qualified competitor for the position in the other company merging with yours. Or the company may be taking this opportunity to find new talent.
- Second, whether you have any alternatives outside the company in case you do decide (or your manager decides for you) that you should leave.
- Third, what will it really be like in the new company post-merger, will you like it, and can you be successful there? Concerns such as these will be particularly pronounced in acquired companies. Even for those in the acquiring company, the deal will create a level of uncertainty not just for each employee but for their families and friends.

I don't want to work for them

"Lots of people left following the acquisition by Procter & Gamble. They perceived moving to P&G as the same thing as moving to another company. They didn't see any difference between moving to P&G or to some other company as in both cases it would be a new company."

Country head of IT, Gillette and then P&G

Remember, if you do plan to leave, you will want to do so before it is public knowledge that you might have been made redundant if you hadn't left. It is usually easier to find a job when you have a job. You certainly have more leverage in negotiations with any prospective employer if they don't know that you are desperate for a job because you don't have one right now. Companies in the midst of an acquisition or merger may be willing to agree that they will not make public your redundancy until after a certain amount of time – sometimes as short as a couple of weeks but more often as long as three months or even longer in some instances. This is the time when you can be looking for a job and the job marketplace will think you are still firmly in your old position. Do be prepared with an answer to the question about why you are leaving, as it is likely that everyone in your industry will know your company is combining with another.

This question about whether you will like the "new" company is critical. Even if they were in the acquirer and it was a much larger company, many survivors find that the new firm is very different from what the old company was like. The culture is likely to change. Not all managers will be the same and they may operate differently: the target will be likely to have some executives placed in the new company and you could be reporting to one of them. Why else would the target have been bought if there wasn't some talent worth retaining?

Need to know what you're in for

"You should gain an understanding of how that company functions and what 'the rules of the game' are. Either you accept these rules and comply with them or you don't accept them and look for a new job."

Manager, consumer products

You may be reassigned. As discussed in Chapter 3, you may also be put through a reapplication process which is painful and insulting – as many employees and managers do not appreciate having to prove to a group of outside consultants that they can do a job that they've been doing for many years. But as important will be the individual work you do day-to-day in the newly combined company.

Between the two organizations, there will have been some redundancies. These may be a significant number, perhaps even as high as one-third, as shown in Figure 2.2 in Chapter 2. However, most (sometimes all) of the work remains to be done; most tasks aren't eliminated from the new company. Combine this with the fact that companies are more efficient at removing employees than removing the necessity for the work that the employees have been doing, and you end up with a situation where the same amount of work in the new company must be done by fewer people. And simultaneously these survivors of the merger process need to learn how the new company operates. Over time you do get more efficient, but it does take time. Yet the period immediately following a merger is one not only where you will be doing your old job, but perhaps someone else's as well ... plus having to learn that person's job, so you won't be working at top speed and the new managers will be demanding perfection as they try to prove that the new organization is better than the old one. If that isn't a recipe for hard work and longer hours, what is?

In a survey of survivors of mergers and acquisitions conducted for this book (see Figure 7.1), it was a very mixed bag as to whether the employees remaining in the company found it better afterwards than before. Work/life balance was least likely to improve (although over half noted no change) and almost twice as many found the culture worse than better. Career issues (promotion prospects, compensation, and benefits) did improve, so clearly there was some reward for those who stayed.

As a result of your most recent experience of an M&A process, were the following aspects of your role the same, better or worse?			
	Better	No change	Worse
Career prospects	49%	38%	13%
Compensation/benefits package	40%	48%	12%
Autonomy	25%	50%	25%
Working environment	28%	40%	31%
Company culture	23%	35%	42%
Work/life balance	11%	55%	33%

Note: Figures may not add to 100% due to rounding

Figure 7.1   How survivors rated their experience with the M&A process
Source: Dickenson and Wood, Cass Business School (2008)

In another survey in 2002, the Chartered Institute of Personnel and Development found that 52.2% of respondents stated that there was a decline in morale of remaining employees and 30.3% said that there was a loss of trust towards the organization among remaining employees after the redundancies took place.

In summary, the survivors of a merger – the "lucky" 85%–90% who weren't made redundant – often reported the following:

• They work harder.
• They have lower morale (principally because of the process whereby many of their long-term colleagues were asked to leave and they haven't yet made the same social connections with their new colleagues).
• They do not understand for a long period what their managers expect of them (and the managers may also be just as much in the dark so can't tell them).
• They do not yet know how the culture in the new company works and whether they will like it (as new cultures often evolve slowly over time).
• They also feel guilty that they have kept their job while others were asked to leave. They may be angry over how their friends were treated when they were made redundant. No

matter how well the news is communicated, being fired is still very stressful and there's little that can be done to sugar-coat the news.

Therefore, knowing this (even if just intuitively) and combined with the possibility of perhaps still losing their job, when many people hear of a possible or actual merger or acquisition, the first reaction is one of panic.

DON'T PANIC

There's a lot to do. The options are not all negative, even if they seem so initially. Start by asking yourself this first question: "Can the merger actually serve as a jump start to a new career?"

In answering this question, stay focused on your own career goals. This is a time to think about yourself first. Do you want to remain with the new company or is this the perfect opportunity to change? As noted above, the merger can often be used as the excuse to move. Fortunately, when you do go looking for a job prospective employers will assume that every merger has the consequence that good people leave (and also, fortunately, it is widely known that the people who leave first are often some of the best and are those with the most external career opportunities; these are the same people who don't want to waste time to wait to see if they are retained).

Jumping ship

"The first group of people left immediately after the announcement of acquisition. Others waited until they received an offer and left with both new jobs *and* remuneration packages."

Treasury analyst, consumer products

Timing is critical at this point in your decision process, as demonstrated in the box below. You clearly do not want to leave the company before you know whether you will like the new organization and whether you may even get a better position once the deal has closed, but you also do not want to be associated with the newly merged company if it fails during or soon after the integration.

Remaining too long may be risky

"... staying also can carry big risks. If the executive ultimately loses his post, being associated with a failed or troubled company can carry a stigma in the job market. Indeed, a recent study indicated that top executives who jumped before a business failed suffered less career damage than peers who stayed to the end. The study, conducted by professors at Indiana University, Texas A&M University, and Tulane University, examined career consequences for executives at banks that failed during the 1980s financial bust in Texas. It found that 54% of senior executives who stayed had to take lower-ranking jobs at their next employer, compared with 41% who bailed. Similarly, 77% of executives who stayed had to change cities for their next job, compared with 23% of jumpers."

Wall Street Journal, *January 22, 2008*

PACKAGES PROVIDED FOR LEAVERS

Perhaps there will be an opportunity to take an attractive redundancy package. Redundancy packages can often be higher immediately after a merger than at other times. The company will have taken financial provisions for such redundancies and will be expecting to pay this out. You will also probably be part of a larger group being made redundant which in some countries triggers a requirement that all people fired be treated similarly and perhaps even with statutory mandated minimum redundancy packages. Most acquirers want to avoid negative publicity during a merger, and offering an attractive redundancy package may help to keep the fired employees quieter than they would be otherwise.

Attractive redundancy packages

"Packages on offer are usually generous and you may find a new role in a company you have dreamed of working for. But this is not a given, so choose wisely considering family situation and friends."

Manager, technology company

A redundancy package would be especially attractive if you were considering leaving anyway. Many companies not only pay for you to leave, but offer at the same time outplacement counseling, retraining, relocation benefits, and other benefits, which were discussed partially in Chapter 3 and will be discussed further below. In most companies, employees made redundant following a merger are also considered "good leavers" and thus keep many of the benefits that they had accrued during their career, such as healthcare and other insurances (at least for some period of time), long-term incentive compensation including share options, and even deferred cash bonuses.

Spotlight: Bankers Trust

Staff preparation in a company being acquired

In 1998, the senior management of Bankers Trust, the eighth largest bank in the USA, knew that it would be acquired. The principal banking regulator in the USA, the Federal

Reserve Board, had told Bankers Trust management that they needed to take steps to improve their capital base and reduce risks, including specifically in their trading books. They were told to look for a strong partner with whom to merge.

Given that management knew that they would be acquired, preparations were made by many in the bank to reduce their personal financial risks. There was some history to this preparation, as revealed by the equity research analysts at Sanford Bernstein.

Only the previous year, in 1997, Bankers Trust had acquired Alex Brown, the oldest investment bank in the USA. At the time of acquisition, it became known that the top 20 executives of Alex Brown had signed special employment contracts with benefits in case the company was acquired. It was also revealed that Bankers Trust had earmarked nearly $300 million over three years for incentive compensation for a group of several hundred key Alex Brown staff employees.

Given this history of retention payments and the expectation that they were to be acquired, it is not surprising that when Deutsche Bank acquired Bankers Trust just under two years later, Bloomberg reported that the chairman of Bankers Trust had a contract with the firm worth $55 million over five years plus $14 million over three years in deferred compensation. It was rumored that his severance package was $100 million when he ultimately left Deutsche Bank only a month after the deal closed in June 1999. The Bankers Trust CFO also left, reputedly with another sizeable package.

It was not only the very top staff who benefited from these retention and redundancy payments. At the time of the acquisition, Deutsche Bank announced that it expected to take a charge of DM 2 billion ($1.2 million) to cover severance payments and set aside DM 700 million (almost $420 million) over three years for retention payments to retain 200 key staff at Bankers Trust.

The decision to leave is an easy one if you are lucky enough to have lined up a new job (or know that you can do so quickly). You still might want to wait around as the situation may yet change – or change again – in your existing company and the conditions may improve to a point where they are better than at your job-offer company. Yet the uncertainty may not be worth it, especially if you can take an attractive redundancy package and "double dip" as some people call it. In some industries, such as banking in the 1990s where there were many mergers or acquisitions, many employees were able to be paid for two or even three jobs simultaneously while actually showing up at work for just one (see the Spotlights on the Deutsche Bank/Bankers Trust acquisition above and below). They could do this because they had a redundancy package from a previous employer who had merged, yet had found work right away in another company.

Most redundancy packages will pay you a set amount for each year you've worked with the company (say, two weeks' compensation for each year of employment). Thus, if you've been at the company for 12 years and have this kind of package, you will be paid (usually in a lump sum) equivalent to 24 weeks, or almost a half year. If you find work elsewhere during this period – and especially if you had been interviewing already and thus had another job at the ready – then you could be pulling down two salaries for that half year.

> **Spotlight: Bankers Trust**
>
> **"Double dipping" at Bankers Trust**
>
> When Deutsche Bank acquired Bankers Trust in 1999 (in the deal announced in late 1998), one of the principal reasons for the acquisition was Bankers Trust's "crown jewel" of investment banking. Bankers Trust was a leader in the technology investment banking area, having itself acquired the oldest investment bank in America, Alex Brown & Sons, founded in Baltimore in 1810. As the acquisition of Alex Brown had only taken place in 1997 and many staff had been given three-year retention bonuses by Bankers Trust, when Deutsche Bank made them redundant, some not only had their redundancy packages related to the Bankers Trust acquisition, but also their retention packages from the Alex Brown acquisition.

You will naturally assume that senior management and the human resources department are taking care first of the people they want to keep in the organization. These are the people who represent the future of the firm. Only after determining how they will incentivize key staff to stay should managers begin to think about what should be done for those who are leaving. Of course, in the best-run deals, these will be simultaneous processes, but management should certainly be focusing more attention on the "keepers" than the "leavers."

This isn't always the case, as discussed earlier, and in many deals the people being made redundant will initially receive the most attention. Those who do want to leave can perhaps use this to their advantage in negotiating a better or quicker deal. If the firm's processes are working properly and the policies, procedures, and selection of the key retained employees are being handled first, the redundancies then become even more important because, if they are not handled properly, there's a chance that their mishandling will contaminate the entire organization. As consultants McKinsey point out, "the best long-term strategy is a very generous severance plan: the cost is high, but good plans have a strongly positive influence on the morale of the remaining employees."

IF YOU DON'T ASK, YOU DON'T GET

Knowing that the company wants you to be happy is helpful knowledge that you can use to your advantage in asking for and possibly receiving an attractive redundancy package. You do retain some leverage over the organization even after you've said that you want to leave, although obviously the higher up in the organization you are, the greater that leverage may be. Lower level employees may find themselves being treated on a group-wide basis as mentioned above, but still retaining some ability to negotiate within somewhat narrower limits. Most executives assume that retention incentives and related expenses will add anywhere from 5% to 10% to the total cost of the acquisition. These costs can be huge: the *Wall Street Journal* reported in May 2008 that had the Microsoft acquisition of Yahoo proceeded, Microsoft had planned to devote $1.5 billion to retaining employees – these funds being available to pay employees not to leave Yahoo for competitors; there would have been an additional amount to pay the people who left for terminating their employment with either of the two companies.

There are steps that you can take on your own as well. If you anticipate that your company will be acquired and that you are at high risk of being made redundant, redundancy insurance may be available. There are important restrictions to these policies, including that you don't know at the time you take out the policy that you will be made redundant and that the redundancy is not voluntary. Offsetting these restrictions are other benefits from these policies, such as providing help with writing your *curriculum vitæ* or résumé, interviewing tips, and even advice about becoming self-employed. If you do feel you are at risk, private unemployment insurance may therefore be worthwhile.

The government will also provide most redundant workers with assistance. This varies widely by country and even within countries (such as by state in the USA or even by city). As with most government benefits, these have limits that are set relatively low compared to most job wages and also have significant restrictions: some include requirements that you must be actively looking for a job and perhaps even the requirement to take a lower level (and lower paying) job if one is offered to you.

OUTPLACEMENT SERVICES

It isn't just cash payments that are given to departing employees. In some cases, the non-cash components of a redundancy package can be even more valuable in the long run than the cash component. One of the most important non-cash benefits, as noted in Chapter 3, is the opportunity to use outplacement services. For example, Cranfield Business School conducted an executive outplacement survey in 1993 and found that 75% of companies in the UK offered outplacement services to its executives who were made redundant, and a study by the American Management Association in the same year reported a figure of 80%, up from only 50% three years earlier. Figures may be even higher today. As shown in Chapter 3, outplacement can be used as a means to ensure that both those who were laid off as well as those retained felt that the firm was treating its employees properly.

> **Value of outplacement services**
>
> "Too many people turn their noses up at working with out-placement providers these days. Many of those losing their jobs this time round may never get back on the treadmill (or might not want to). Outplacement personnel are ideally placed to help market professionals open their eyes to alternative career opportunities."
>
> *Reader comment in* Here is the City, *a London-based news and careers website*

There has been a shift from the traditional use of outplacement services offered only to executive level employees, to employees at lower levels of the organization. Outplacement provides career counseling and related services to individual departing employees or groups of employees. These related services can include some of the same items as with the examples of employment insurance above (assistance with writing *curricula vitæ* and résumés, training in interviewing skills, and information about changing careers and industries), but also additional help such as psychometric testing, provision of an "office" where an ex-employee can work during the initial period of redundancy, secretarial services including photocopiers and subscription databases such as up-to-date lists of companies currently hiring, and even just a place to meet other people recently made redundant who can share their advice on their current job searches or career changes. These outplacement activities can take place on a one-to-one basis with an expert coach, be group sessions, or maybe some combination of the two where some activities are conducted with an individual coach and others in larger groups.

The intended message of outplacement, from the merging businesses' perspective, is to show that the employer cares about their employees, including those leaving because of the merger.

Because there are very good business reasons that companies provide this service (with the assumption that its use will help to improve the corporate image with employees who are made redundant and even those who remain), it is possible for senior employees to request this benefit even if it isn't initially offered. Knowing that your company may want you to go "quietly and happily" does give you some leverage in asking for a good outplacement package.

Of course, your company may not provide such outplacement services and may not be persuaded to do so even if you ask. You might nevertheless consider paying for it yourself. However, at a time when you are concerned about your finances, this may not be a cost that you want to incur, so consider as well whether friends or even family can fill this role – assuming they can separate the objective external perspective that is necessary to provide the appropriate professional advice from their own personal relationship with you.

DECISION TO STAY: WHAT NOW?

For the remainder of the book, let's assume that you do not really want to leave the newly merged company and collect your redundancy cash or change careers. What should you do? There are some survival tips aimed at improving your chances of keeping your job – or perhaps getting a better job in the newly combined company. Starting with suggestions about planning a defensive strategy, this book will then discuss the importance of building and using your network of contacts, some ideas about attitude and self-promotion (including using company politics to your advantage), and lastly the need to be a performer during this period of transition.

CHAPTER 8

DEFENSE IS THE BEST OFFENSE

Agood defense supports the best offense. Survival does imply a need for self-preservation. Although there are those who can and will benefit from a merger or acquisition and exit at the end of the deal process with a better job, more money, or both, for most employees success will be measured by whether you can merely keep a job with the company. As will be discussed in the next chapter, you will certainly need to marshal the support of internal colleagues and expand your external network, but for most of the time, you will be handling the chaos of the merger largely on your own. That is the focus of this chapter.

You're on your own

"We're all self-employed people: you have to have your own marketing plan for your own employment."

Chief operating officer, information technology company

DON'T THINK YOUR OWN BOSS WILL TAKE CARE OF YOU

You may believe that your manager will take care of you. In fact, he or she may truly have your best interests in mind and may even tell you that he or she will make sure that you and the rest of your team will be retained post-merger. "Don't worry," you'll be told, "I know this company well, I know what's happening, and I can assure you that we're safe."

Don't believe it.

It will be wonderful if it does turn out to be true, but depending 100% on your boss is very, very risky. You can't rely on anyone – but yourself. As noted earlier in the book, the research shows that during the period of uncertainty surrounding a merger, everyone – from the hourly-paid factory worker to the CEO – can be expected to be looking out for him or herself first.

Despite best intentions, your boss needs to clarify his or her own position first before he or she can be of much assistance to others. Until they are certain that they are "safe" in the new organization, they will have very limited ability to control any of the post-merger decisions – and certainly cannot guarantee anything before they receive a firm appointment themselves. Depending on where you're located in the firm (front office or back office (the former usually get determined first as noted in Chapter 5), high in the organization chart or low (again, the former are decided more quickly), etc), it may be a while before your boss knows what's happening to him or her and the group. The decisions about whether your boss is retained may even be made several times – first it looks like he or she's staying, but then something changes and your boss is on his or her way out, or vice versa.

Candid self-appraisal needed

"Staff should assess their worth to the new organization and the chances that their role can be easily filled by others."

Back office employee, technology company

Thus, your boss may be facing the axe or just fears that he or she is at significant risk of being asked to leave the firm, and therefore unable to focus on anything, including your position. Your boss may even be in more danger than you, as the redundancy risk is higher the further up the organization you are, as noted in Chapter 5.

As with everyone else in the organization, your boss can be expected to be looking out for him or herself first. So, not only is it dangerous to put your trust in your manager in the early days after you're first told about the merger or acquisition, but if you do solely rely on him or her, you're likely to be missing valuable time when you should be taking proactive steps of your own. These include preparing and acting on your own job defense plan – including contingency plans in case your boss is fired. Such a "Plan B" (*What to do if my boss is fired and his promises about my future job are worthless*) should be developed simultaneously with your "Plan A" (*Follow my boss into the new company because he said I was critical to the new team that he's been asked to lead*) and implemented only if Plan A falls apart.

Personal action plans

"Do not rely on support from anyone other than yourself particularly as your existing support network may not be effective within the new organization. Develop a personal action plan with built-in contingencies for potential developments."

Chief operating officer, large European bank

Most organizations make the new management decisions from the very top first, and then work their way downwards by management layer. Best practice is to announce a new layer of management every four to six weeks following the deal announcement, with the very top managers announced at the time the deal is first publicized. This is, for example, what The Bank of New York and Mellon Financial planned and achieved in their merger in 2007. Therefore, if retained, your boss is likely to be in a position to help you eventually, but unless you are reporting to that very top layer, it could be a month or longer for him or her to be in a position which is useful to you.

Look out for your boss being reassigned to a position where they cannot use you and therefore a position where they cannot provide you with support. A merger or acquisition can be the catalyst for major reorganizations including moving managers and staff into new (for them) groups or possibly into newly formed departments that didn't even exist in either one of the two merging companies. If it is likely that your boss will be moved, you should put even more effort into forming new networks and your own defense.

No answers while in limbo

"What was I to do? All the good people were leaving, my boss couldn't tell me the status of my job, and those that hadn't left kept asking me what was going to happen to them."

Junior manager, marketing

Politics also plays a role in the decision as to whether your boss will remain with the company. With many mergers, there is an attempt to pick a similar number of staff at each level from both organizations. (This is less frequent with acquisitions than mergers, as, in the latter, both companies are supposed to be equals or close to equals but with acquisitions there is no such pretension.) Yet rarely are both companies equal to each other in everything. In trying to fulfill this "myth" of egalitarianism, some of the better managers may be sacrificed (that is, made redundant) in order to get the numbers evenly matched in picking people from both organizations. Your boss may be clearly better than his or her counterpart at the other company but could still not get the better job in the integration of the two organizations. Of course, these political decisions may apply to your level as well, so beware especially of the cascading effect of redundancies where one senior person is fired, those reporting directly to him or her therefore leave or are also fired, and so on down the organization chart. Other types of political issues and how best to play the political game are covered later in Chapter 11.

There's also the possibility that your manager simply knows even less than you about what's going on in the company – particularly if official lines of communication break down, as they often do in the uncertainty and chaos following an M&A announcement. You may think that those above will know more about what's going on. They certainly should in an ideal situation and if the company has developed an effective communications roll-out plan. However, many companies haven't developed such plans and even those firms that do will find that they have difficulty implementing them as planned because events change too rapidly (including the unexpected departure of key executives) and the intended communication is out of date or wrong before it can be sent.

If you've been diligent in building your own communications network and if you have begun trading information about the deal both internally and externally (as will be suggested in the next chapter), then it is possible that your boss (unless they are actively doing the same) will know less than you about the deal and the decisions being made about who will be retained and fired. In 2007, a report by The Forum Corporation, a performance improvement consulting firm, found that 64% of those involved in leading change during an M&A deal claimed that they had not been given enough preparation by their organization's senior management. So if only one-third of that group of "insiders" to the deal feels they have enough information, unless your boss is one of the few in that group, it isn't even necessarily your boss's fault that he or she is unable to provide the guidance on what is happening or how to deal with the changes.

What else can be done if your boss hasn't a clue? Approach more senior executives directly to understand how the transaction could impact your position, suggested one back office junior manager in an interview. Although you may not be able to do this without offending your boss (and his or her support may be critical later to your own survival), sometimes merger and acquisition situations will provide opportunities to discuss the deal with managers above your own boss. Senior executives or even the CEO may have "town hall" meetings to discuss the merger, there could be smaller sessions with other executives or perhaps with the transition and integration teams, and there may even be a blog or "Ask the CEO" website that solicits candid comments and questions from staff, sometimes anonymously. Use all these available forums.

Lastly, don't hesitate to talk with your boss about the deal. Some people find it difficult to be direct, but it will be critically important to your own future so you might just have to take a deep breath, walk into his or her office, and ask your questions. It isn't easy to ask anyone and especially your manager directly whether he or she expects to stay with the firm. You may just be given the official answer of "Of course I will" that the managers have been instructed to say, but then again you might be lucky and get a candid answer. It is important to try at least to understand how decisions will be made above you, as the same or very similar processes are likely to be used shortly at your level.

PREPARE FOR THE WORST

Even if you're lucky enough to have a boss who is knowledgeable about the deal, and willing and able to help you retain your position in the newly merged company, it's still critical to have the "Plan B" noted above, as the job in the new company may be less secure than you thought and, as also noted above, your boss may yet decide to leave the company because of the merger. Remember as well from Chapter 2 that most M&A deals go sour after the immediate hype at announcement or closing, so your job may disappear even if you are fortunate enough to start the transition or post-merger integration period with a firm position (see "Most fail – so you can win the battle but lose the war" in that same chapter).

Have alternatives planned

"The 'truth' in any M&A situation will only emerge over time. Adapt to it and keep an open mind and have a plan b, c, d, e, etc."

Senior advisor, bank

"Your name will always be on a list somewhere," says one managing director with a Swiss bank, referring to the chances of being made redundant after an acquisition or a merger has been announced. Therefore, when rumors do appear, take them seriously – especially if your company is the smaller one being acquired. Even if you think you're a survivor, take defensive action on the home front such as cutting unnecessary personal expenditure, reducing debts, and saving money. Now is not the time to remodel the kitchen, move house, or buy that second home you'd seen while on holiday. The more stretched your finances, the more important budgeting of this kind will be. Uncertainty about finances will also make it more difficult to move through the psychological steps of dealing with the merger.

You'll want to determine just how likely you are to be made redundant and how seriously to take the rumors that your group may be (or is) at risk. "Don't think you're safe!" warned one banker, while another manager from the accountancy industry simply advised, "There are no guarantees." When the managing director of a Bulgarian telecommunications company first heard unconfirmed reports that his company might be a target of the much larger British Telecom (BT), he started off by looking at the BT annual report and website to see where the overlaps might be with his team in order to understand the relative strengths of his people versus those in the division of BT currently operating in the area. Phone calls were made and clients contacted to get some further intelligence. He ultimately concluded – correctly – that there were few overlaps and his group was likely to be retained intact (which they were), but his analysis could have shown the opposite if the acquirer had been stronger in his country already.

Take control

"You have to take control of your own destiny. If you are not allowed to or if management has plans for you that you do not agree with, make sure you have a contingency plan."

Sales manager, finance firm

Call headhunters (especially those who have contacted you in the past). Update your résumé or *curriculum vitæ*, and make sure you circulate it. Read the job advertisements. The sooner you start putting feelers out the better – the danger is that the market becomes flooded by job applicants, noted a senior manager of an acquired IT/telecoms firm, because others in your company will be doing the same once they get over the initial shock. Getting organized in this way has an extra side benefit, as it may also help reduce your personal anxiety about the situation and start the process of regaining control.

If rumors appear or your company is actually in play (and even if it isn't but you think your company could be acquired), have your employment contract revised to include a golden or silver parachute, if possible. You may not have a package worth $100 million as shown in the example in the previous chapter of the CEO of Bankers Trust when it was acquired by Deutsche Bank in 1999, but even much more reasonable and modest sums can be helpful if you do find yourself jobless because of an M&A deal. It isn't just the golden parachutes either. If you are made redundant, there is often some negotiation possible on other aspects of the leaving package, especially for those higher up in the organization. Importantly, too, as a manager whose media/ entertainment firm was subject to a hostile takeover said to us: "Don't take it personally. No job is ever safe in a weak and failing company."

OFFENSIVE DEFENSE

You can't afford to be passive. You must take defensive action to be prepared for the worst if your own best efforts to retain a job fall short − or perhaps if you're just unlucky despite having taken all the steps that you should have. Similarly, passivity through reliance on others is risky − as they are not only likely to be looking out first for themselves, but may also not be in as strong a position as you are, even if you don't feel particularly in control yourself. This is as much a mindset, as will be shown in Chapter 10, as it is the result of specific defensive actions.

CHAPTER 9

NETWORKS AND CONTACTS

It's important to use your network of contacts to gather intelligence and to provide assistance. The tendency for many when a deal is announced is to put their heads down, ignore the deal, and just work. There may even be the feeling that working diligently in the trenches is safer than if you put your head up and then get noticed and possibly shot (read: fired). In fact, the opposite is usually true. You need to be noticed. There will be lists prepared. The first list is those who are essential to the post-merger company and the second is those who aren't. Often this second list is merely those not on the first list. To get on the first list, you therefore need to be a performer, but you'll need to have information about what's going on so that you know exactly what you should be doing to get noticed. The official lines of communication usually aren't terribly reliable in the middle of the chaos of most M&A deals. You also need support.

The other dangerous tendency is for employees of the acquirer to be complacent. They feel, because they are from the company in control of the deal, that they do not need to be as active in protecting their jobs as employees of the target must be. They may feel secure, but this is definitely a false sense of safety, as noted in Chapter 5 about who is more likely to be retained post-acquisition. There will probably be some managers and employees from the target chosen over people from the acquirer. In that chaos following the announcement of an M&A deal, excellent managers and staff at both the target and acquirer will voluntarily depart, as many just don't want to have to sit through the turmoil and uncertainty that will take place for months, if not years. These departures will provide additional opportunities for those who stay.

At risk in the acquirer

"During an acquisition early in my career I assumed that because the business I worked for was the acquirer my existing management (with whom I had a great relationship) would remain. Not the case, the acquired business's senior management took over. My network and experience meant nothing. I had to rebuild my reputation."

Manager, finance firm

INFORMATION IS POWER

Reaching out to others will hopefully provide you with new information that your group of close colleagues doesn't have, but your group will likewise know some things which they don't. As with external people, you can therefore horse-trade information with them, and also encourage them to seek information from yet other teams. Viral information sharing will result. Some of the data that will filter back will be useful, but there will also be wrong information and even dangerous gossip. Careful sifting of the data is therefore critical, which you can do by having multiple sources of information and trying hard to understand how each source got the information they did and how the findings relate to each other.

Importance even of rumor

"Pay attention to the grapevine. Any advance warning of which way the wind is blowing is critical. You don't want to be backing the wrong horse if you can avoid it."

Partner, financial services firm

Since the time when a merger or acquisition is taking place is one of uncertainty, if not even total confusion, you will have difficulty determining what is rumor and truth. Gossip will be rampant throughout both companies – not just about the deal itself (when it will close, what the organization chart will look like, which product lines will be retained, etc.) but also the most important topic on everyone's mind: "Who will go and who will stay?" Each employee will be trying to determine whether to leave now or see the deal through and, if they do remain, whether there's a real possibility of landing an even better position than that which they currently have.

Using the deal to get ahead

"A better question might be: if you want to stay with the new organization, how can you take advantage of the evolving dynamics in a situation where the normal information/intelligence flow has been severely disrupted (that is, trusted relationships and previous processes are no longer reliable)?"

Technology consultant, Santa Fe, New Mexico

You will need to determine who has the information that will allow you to make an informed decision. Who is most likely to know what is really going on? Who can you trust? Who will help you? And what can you give to them in return, because this is a time when everyone is seeking information and they will want to know what you have found out as well.

Importance of networks up the hierarchy

"At senior levels the importance of internal networks and politics is far more critical in determining if an individual survives and/or benefits from an M&A situation. At junior levels, bar making clear your compensation requirements, the need to rely on politics is far less significant."

Finance employee, finance firm

THE VALUE OF YOUR NETWORK

Your own network internal to the company and externally among friends and business associates is critical both to gather intelligence about what is to happen and also to gain support as decisions are made. Outsiders should not be underestimated in terms of what they might know about the deal. Many employees ignore this fact, relying solely on the people they know inside the firm.

Often, those outside the company – such as executive search firms, employment agencies, consultants, clients, and suppliers – will know more about certain aspects of the merger, be more objective, have a clearer perspective, and be less likely to be affected emotionally. These external groups all have a vested interest in knowing what is happening now that the companies have announced a deal. Outsiders with linkages to the two companies that therefore want and need to retain their business will themselves be doing whatever they can to gather information aggressively to aid their own planning and future relationship with the new company post-merger. You can both assist them with this in terms of telling them what's happening (assuming that you have the authority and clearance to discuss the deal externally), and at the same time trade information with them to get a perspective from an outside source.

One of the most important groups of outsiders, as discussed in Chapter 6, will be the consultants, investment bankers, lawyers, accountants, and public relations professionals who are working with senior management on the deal itself. These advisors may even be responsible for helping management select the employees to be retained (see Chapter 3).

Networking with the deal advisors

"If possible, gently persuade outside advisors to keep your profile in front of the decision-makers. Investment bankers, lawyers, consultants, etc. will often carry more weight in the mind of buyers than the 'acquired' team. It doesn't hurt for you to network a bit with these folks and suggest they 'put in a good word' for you."

Rich Aiello, Welsh, Carson, Anderson & Stowe, private equity investment firm

---

Networking externally will also help you to gain greater visibility should it all go awry and you wish or need to move employers. Benefits of this external network can also extend well beyond the period when you're redundant. Emphasizing the longer-term value of such efforts, one of our survey respondents said: "The network that I established at that time [of the merger] served me well then and is the most valuable contact list I have now, several years later." This is especially true of headhunters, who will know a lot about an industry and who could be helpful again in the future.

Networks and new jobs

"Network aggressively and be very proactive about looking for a new job. The merged company will either want to retain you or not – you have nothing to lose by looking for new employment and a job offer will strengthen your internal negotiating position."

General manager, finance industry

Whether internal or external, you need to let your network know about your accomplishments, talents, and what you've done for the company. This is not the time for false modesty. You want and need a job. Your network can help.

Need for continual networking

"When I look back over the years and several mergers and acquisitions, I can't overstate the importance of networking. This includes headhunters and social networks, not just people in the company and industry. It's a mistake throughout your career to ever be 'too tired' to do socializing with the intent to build your network or to strengthen it. If you're not networking at least twice a week, then you're not doing it enough. Establish connections *before* you need a job!"

Vice-president, information technology, European bank

You need all of the "friends" you can get. One reason is that you don't know who will be asked to assess you or your department's performance, for example. Another reason is that you never know who will be the one to steer you to a particularly useful piece of information that will turn out to be critical to your decision about whether to stay or leave.

Internally, you will need to reach out to people beyond your traditional network of close colleagues. Go outside your department and even into the other company. Why? Because your close colleagues are likely to have the same information – and sources – as you. Talking just to your colleagues will only serve to reinforce opinions that you already have.

Expanding your network

"Quickly build a new network of contacts in the emerging organization and meet the appointed managers that will influence the future organization relevant to your role and functions. Do not leave this to your superiors, integration teams, or HR."

Chief operating officer, large European bank

Another reason to contact these other people within the firm is that you can use it to promote the good work for the company that you and your team have done. This does need to be done subtly, of course, as discussed later in Chapter 11 on self-promotion. Similarly, ask others for help beyond the mere sharing of information – but offer to help them as well. Many people assume that asking for help is a sign of weakness or incompetence, but it can be a powerful tool in building your network, even in the midst of a merger. Additionally, by asking for help, you compliment someone: you're telling them that you think they can do something well (or that they know something you don't) and that you value what they will say.

Networking reflects well on you

"Network as much as possible and be very aggressive – during the merger process senior executives are usually looking for confident and aggressive employees to fill key roles."

Manager, IT/telecommunications firm

USING YOUR NETWORK

Using networks means recruiting others into the battle, suggests Jeffrey Sonnenfeld, Professor of Management Practice at the Yale School of Management and co-author of *Firing Back: How Great Leaders Rebound after Career Disasters*. In his book, published in 2007, he reminds us of the old adage: "It's not what you know, it's who you know." The acquaintances – and they are likely to be people that you meet only once or twice a year or even less often – will provide support in two areas: giving you the social and emotional support that you need to keep stable (and more often this is provided by those in your circle who are close friends and family) and helping you to find a new job if you need one (or even just a potential new job that makes you feel more confident in negotiating for something better at your newly merged company).

You need to identify how best to contact your network and when to ask for help. Generally, you should divide your existing network into three groups:

1. Close friends and colleagues: These are the people both internally and externally who you know very well: childhood and university friends, neighbors, and colleagues (current and former) with whom you have developed a social and not just business relationship. A good test to determine whether someone is really in this group is to think about them in terms of what is called the "bother test." That is, if you can call them every few days and they wouldn't be bothered (which means that they still answer your calls and respond to your emails), then they belong in this group. You can, therefore, keep checking with them as to whether there is any news relating to your situation, and these people anyway would in all likelihood initiate feeding you information as they uncover it. You can also ask them for help, and they will do everything

they can to assist. If you think that they will be "bothered" by such frequent contact or requests for help, they belong in the next group.

2. Business associates and occasional friends: These are people who you know well but who, if you call on them too often, will stop responding. They may be friends or former colleagues who you don't see very often, or even other parents at your son's or daughter's Saturday soccer club. You can, therefore, usually contact them once every few weeks, but no more frequently. Simple requests for help (e.g. asking them to check with someone else to confirm something you've heard) are OK, but it is unlikely they will drop everything to assist you, as people in the first group would. You know people in the second group directly and normally retain contact with them (outside of the ritual of sending Christmas cards, for example), or else they belong in the third and final group.

3. Other acquaintances: This group is basically all the other people who know you personally. They are people who you've met once or perhaps only see a few times a year (sometimes less) but who would recognize your name if their secretary put a note on their desk to call you back. You may keep in touch with them electronically through MySpace or Facebook. You typically have just one shot with them: you cannot go back to them more frequently, and the requests must be simple for them to carry out, as they don't know you well enough to spend a tremendous amount of time or effort assisting you.

It is the latter group of people who can be surprisingly useful, as the first two categories are likely to think more like you and, as noted earlier, have the same information sources as you. In one famous study by Mark Granovetter published in the *American Journal of Sociology* in 1973 entitled "The Strength of Weak Ties," he found that of those people who found new jobs through the use of a contact, 17% were found through people they saw at least twice a week, 56% were found through people they saw at least once a year, and 28% through distant acquaintances who they saw less than once a year (people they knew at school but who weren't close friends, former co-workers, and the like). Note that more jobs were found through these distant acquaintances than the close friends and colleagues they saw several times a week. The socially networked age of Facebook and LinkedIn may have changed this, but the general principle remains about the power of "distant acquaintances."

It is usually more likely that you will find support from those who know you or about you within your chosen field, than from people in an unrelated industry. These ties within your industry can be very tight and, using the concepts described above, much closer than you may think.

Your boss is part of your network as well. Everyone knows this, but doesn't necessarily use their boss as they should during a merger (although do note the caveat, as was discussed in the previous chapter, that your manager may know less than you do about the deal). Coattails are important. If your boss is successful in landing a good position in the newly combined company, then you have an excellent chance of staying with him or her if you have been a supportive and consistent performer. As one head of legal said when discussing a situation where his company was acquired by a much larger company but where he landed the new head of legal position because the acquiring company's equivalent was near retirement, "People who had worked with me before or knew me, stayed. It didn't feel for us so much like a takeover."

BROADENING YOUR NETWORK

There is yet a fourth group of individuals not currently in your network but who could be useful indirectly. This is the "third-party contacts" list: that is, friends–of-a-friend, a business associate one of your colleagues knows, etc. LinkedIn may be one example of a way to find these contacts, but you must be creative in finding other ways as well. Generally speaking, these "third-party contacts" (or the so-called "weak ties" which Granovetter talks about) are unlikely to know you yet. In order to contact them, you need to drop someone else's name into the request that you send them and hope that your friend or colleague is as well known to them as they claim to be. These "friends-of-a-friend" will then help you or not, depending on how well they do know your contact and if your friend was willing to speak up on your behalf. This group of people can be huge.

You no doubt have heard that almost anyone in the world can be connected to anyone else through only six degrees of separation. This was first described in an article by Stanley Milgram in 1969 and was summarized by Sonnenfeld and Ward in their book as follows: "With a colleague, Milgram selected a person in Boston and then selected people at random from the state of Nebraska. Milgram gave the people in Nebraska a document and asked them to send it to someone they knew personally who would be more likely to advance the progress of the document toward the recipient in Boston. As each recipient passed on the document, they also mailed a postcard to Milgram so that he could trace the number of steps between these two randomly selected individuals, some thirteen hundred miles apart. Milgram found that, on average, it took only 5.2 steps to reach the recipient in Boston!"

If it worked for Milgram in 1969 by using the postal service, think how much faster and more effective this would be in today's world of instant messaging.

SCAN WIDELY

It is difficult at any time to know who might be of help, so it is important to use the shotgun approach rather than the rifle in both gathering information and seeking help. To continue with the metaphors, "don't put all your eggs in one basket." Support may come from an unlikely place. Conversely, a promising lead may go cold. Be careful about making enemies – there's always a chance you might need that person as a supporter, but more importantly perhaps, you don't want that person someday negatively influencing a decision about your future.

Multiple sponsors

"You need multiple sponsors who will support you. Three is ideal. You do not want to be resting everything on one person and he's the wrong one."

Chief operating officer, Swiss investment bank

Especially at senior levels you may be tempted to withdraw for another reason: lack of prestige. For many people, if not most, one critical way we define ourselves is by our job: where we work, what we do at work, and which level or position in the organization we currently occupy. If your job is uncertain and possibly even eliminated because two companies are merging, people who do define themselves through their job will also feel uncertain and insecure. They may even hide their pain – and shame, in their own eyes – out of sight of friends, family, and perhaps from their business acquaintances. However, an M&A deal is the time when everyone affected needs to use all the help they can get. Call in chips. Go out of your way to know even more people. Swallow your pride. Don't hesitate to ask for help.

CHAPTER 10

ATTITUDE COUNTS

Now you think about the deal can either help or hinder your success in finding a job in the new company. As discussed in Chapter 4, you almost can't avoid progressing through a number of stages of emotions about the deal: starting with disbelief, moving through to anger, acceptance, and finally even the possibility of excitement when the full potential of the deal is clear and your role in the new company is more certain.

Attitude affects the outcome

"I strongly believe surviving a company merger is primarily determined by an individual's attitude and constructive consideration of opportunities that the merger creates. The outcome may result in remaining with the newly formed organization or making a conscious career change decision but either of these can be viewed as personal survival."

Chief operating officer, large European bank

At least you've got good company, because everyone in the firm will be going through the same stages, although at different paces. Through better knowledge about what is happening and the application of the suggestions in this book, you may be able to speed up the process for yourself. If, as you now do, you know that you can rely on your network and that you are well prepared for the worst "just in case," then you should be more confident than others and should, therefore, be able to move more quickly at least to the acceptance stage than those around you. As said to us by one survivor of more than a few mergers and acquisitions who also was the architect of a number of deals, it is necessary to "keep focus on what's best for the organization." He noted that this is frequently very tough to do, especially with all of the personal uncertainty about the job, but the acquirer's executives and their senior integration team can, more often than not, see through all of the personal jockeying for jobs and will appreciate and value a willingness to put personal interests aside to "take one for the team." If you do this properly, the personal issues may take care of themselves.

Thus you need not only change your own perceptions of how you see the merger or acquisition to help you deal with the chaos yourself, but you can also affect the perception that others have of you and especially the perceptions of the managers who will be deciding who to retain in the company. You want them to select you, of course, and having the right attitude about the deal should help.

BE POSITIVE AND OPEN ABOUT THE NEW COMPANY

Nobody likes a complainer. If they have a choice, few people will choose to be around those who can't say a good word about their company and their work. No one really wants to work long term with someone who hangs on to or longs for the past, someone who can't stop reminding people why things were better in the old organization (even if they were). Yes, "misery loves company" (and the period immediately following a deal announcement can truly be miserable for most people in the company) – but not all the time.

Keep it positive

"Don't be negative: look for opportunities that may arise and position yourself accordingly."

Middle manager, engineering/manufacturing company

You need to be future oriented and focus on what the new organization needs, not what's been lost in the company that no longer exists. There's potential created by every acquisition or merger, but that potential is only realized through the very hard work of each and every employee. Management will know this, even if they don't do M&A deals very often. They will want people on their future team who can contribute to the firm and buy into the newly created organization, structure, and strategy. "Think ahead to the post-merger situation and make friends with your new team," suggested a board member of a professional services firm.

Start living the new organization

"Quickly change your own state of mind from living the existing organizational culture, values and objectives to living the future state of the new organization. Even if this does not occur 'formally' within the existing organization it is key that this change of state is achieved at the individual level, treat every day as a new job in a new company. This will require investigation and research into the new organization that is itself a positive activity. Don't defend or justify existing processes and practices unless there is certainty that they will fit and benefit the new organization."

Chief operating officer, large European bank

Granted, senior management may be slow in communicating this vision for the new company, but when it does become clear how it will develop, if you want to stay with the firm you need to embrace it while contributing to making changes to improve it, if you're in a position to have such influence.

Don't whine

"Be seen to be proactive. Don't whinge. But don't be too aggressive, as you need to be a team player."

Partner, hedge fund

If you do stay, whether by luck or your own effort and attitude, be focused on the future and what the new organization needs. From the company's perspective, the deal itself – the selection of the firm to be acquired or choosing a merger partner plus details such as the cost of the target and how they're paid – will not alone determine the success of the deal. The acquisition or merger is only successful if the post-deal period is one in which the people in the new company come together and work to make sure that the strategy behind the deal is implemented. This is usually neither quick nor easy and involves constant readjustment. It requires everyone pulling. Just as in tug-of-war, there will be many forces pulling in the opposite direction to undo the deal: competitors trying to lure away clients and the best employees, simple organizational inertia, unseen problems in integration (such as systems that are more difficult to combine than anticipated, people who just can't work together, or problems that should have been uncovered prior to the deal agreement but that remained hidden until after the deal was done), and unforeseen changes in the economy or marketplace. This is why those who remain with the company – or want to remain with the company – must sign up to a long period of hard work to make the deal successful. They must be open to new ideas.

Work with, not against, the firm

"It's very easy to get caught up in the high-uncertainty/high-anxiety discourse in the business, joining in and amplifying rumors, playing the 'ain't-it-awful' game. More often than not, in my experience, those people who rise above the scare-mongering and self-preservation to participate in creating the new organization, and bring others along with them, are likely to do better in the long term."

Alexandra Stubbings, specialist in organizational identity and culture change, Ashridge Consulting

---

A positive outlook about yourself and your place in the company can also be important in easing your own anxieties about work and the merger. The negatives about the merger may be the factors most often discussed at the beginning, as people do feel anger about having to leave behind the organizations they knew and with which they were comfortable, even if they didn't enjoy the work they did previously. "The devil you know versus the devil you don't," as one marketing director reminded us about this reaction to a pending deal. The "focus on the positive" is not just wishful thinking, because, as noted above, it can truly contribute to the success of the deal – or, conversely if the negative rumors and discussion do not come to an end, they will become a self-fulfilling prophecy as good employees leave and those who remain don't put in the effort to make the deal work.

Benefits of the right attitude

"Seek to make the merger work: don't fight it. You have much more to gain with a positive attitude."

Manager, engineering company

It will be especially rewarding if you can help others through this difficult period as well, and this again is not just a

Pollyanna-ish attitude about making you feel better but can be a key part of your own personal survival strategy to gain further support from your network in the organization. Perhaps this is also why a number of people interviewed in the survey of merger survivors (Figure 1.1 in Chapter 1) recommended that you "maintain a sense of humor about the situation."

Support others

"I want to note that the whole company was in crisis at that moment. Overall it was a complete mess. People didn't understand what their tasks were. Employees felt stress as well. As a result personnel were disoriented, embarrassed, and devoid of motivation. My main task was to 'give a shoulder to cry on' to employees from both sides."

Treasury manager, consumer products company

Lastly, whining and complaining is often a trap into which some employees from the target company fall. Many employees were proud to be working in the old company. Many had been there for years and had seen the company grow and succeed, even if the final years may not have been the most successful and led to the need to be acquired. They find it difficult to let go and accept the fact that they are now part of another company and that their former employer was sold, in some cases to a competitor. These are the people who are more likely to keep referring back to the way things were done in the old company.

Time to move on

"Once you've decided to stay with the new company, you've got to move on and no longer wish you were with the old organization. For a lot of people, the acquisition was a time of bereavement. They could never get over it."

Senior department manager, London-based bank

BE FLEXIBLE

"Be flexible" is the simple recommendation of a managing director of a bank who had been in five acquisitions so far in his career. He found that to remain each time, he had to change with the organizations. He concluded that trying to hold onto his existing job – and even defending the need for his "old" job to be retained within the new organizational structure – was a recipe for redundancy. The new organization will be different. Jobs will be redefined and often must be changed as businesses formerly separate are combined. The company may even be using the merger or acquisition to redefine the industry and the way that work is done in that business.

Accept there may be constant change

"We sold our business twice in 36 months, with both sales requiring me to move city."

Partner, private equity firm

Be willing to move or change jobs. In Chapter 5, flexibility was shown to be one of the critical factors enabling one to be chosen to remain. The best positions (or at least those retained in the new organization) may be in a different location or department. Headquarters jobs may face particular upheaval and the organization may be seeking different skills. Show that you are adaptable to a new corporate culture, manager, travel, job requirements, hours, or other business practices. In fact, it is even better to move beyond mere adaptability to a point where you are helping to define the changes necessary for the organization to realize the full potential of the merger. Just as a positive and open attitude is necessary to be successful in the new company, you should even try to see if you can get to the point where you can influence and embrace the changes taking place.

This is true even if the merger is, in your mind, a mistake. Many a deal that should have succeeded has failed – the success rate of mergers demonstrates this. But many deals that should have failed could have been made to succeed. There are opportunities to "make a silk purse out of a sow's ear," advised one senior executive. These are deals that were done for the wrong reasons: the motivation for the board and CEO merely to be bigger (often called "management hubris"), me-too deals where one company tries to copy a competitor's successful deal, takeovers where there has been inadequate planning and due diligence so that the acquiring company doesn't really understand what it has bought, acquisitions where the price paid for the target is too high or just too expensive for the bidder to absorb, or deals where the cultures of the two companies are so different that it would take tremendous effort to bring the two together.

Even if you find yourself in deals that you think are doomed to fail, strong effort on your part – and many other employees, of course, although you may even be the one to inspire some of them – can turn these bad deals into if not successful deals at least not disasters. This does require a willingness to be flexible about the necessary changes and your role with them.

Willingness to change position

"I was open to the changes and considered alternative roles to further develop my skills and career. I saw it as a learning opportunity and experience in a new role. Do not be precious of your existing role and title."

Director of finance, local health board, England

Equally, don't be afraid to use the situation to make significant progress within the merged organization. You don't have merely to maintain your position or level. To paraphrase Sir Winston Churchill, "in adversity is opportunity." The high level of uncertainty when the deal is announced and in the period immediately following will allow some people to advance in the organization if they are willing to act quickly, be flexible, and have ideas about how to reorganize the work. One manager told us that he went from "managing 'two men and a dog' to having a department of 60 staff" in the newly combined company when his firm was acquired. Going one step further (principally for directors and other senior managers), it may also be a good time to secure a pay rise or bonus in return for active commitment to the new organization. As discussed earlier, retention payments are often available to staff who are "too valuable to lose."

Be careful that you don't aim too high, however. Be realistic. That is not to say that you shouldn't go for it, but remember that the assessment process will be even more rigorous for a promotion than for just keeping your job. As shown in the box below, some people have managed to make the most out of the turmoil of a deal – and landed that plum position while others were fired – only to be "found out" within months and then asked to leave. Perhaps if they had been willing just to continue in their old position, they would still be employed.

Aiming too high

"An Assistant Director of Finance applied for the Director of Finance position following a merger of two hospitals. This request clearly showed that she had a lack of insight about her ability and reputation. She left the organization within six months."

Finance director, hospital

HALF EMPTY OR HALF FULL?

Your success with the company following the deal is as much up to you as it is to the company. You may be more in control than first appears. If you act as if the deal will fail for the company, you contribute to its possible failure – and your own. The opposite is also true. Unless you are the CEO or another very senior executive in the firm, it is unlikely that you will have so much of an impact as to cause the overall success or failure of the deal, but you certainly can help to control whether you are personally a survivor or not – and if a survivor then whether you maintain your level in the company or even get a promotion.

CHAPTER 11

THE POLITICS
OF SELF-PROMOTION

W hen a deal is announced, most employees will be tremendously distracted and even preoccupied with determining their future. Others in the company will be slacking off as this is a time when morale generally declines in an organization and people spend hours swapping rumors.

For those who want to be selected to remain with the company, this is the time to pull out all the stops and produce. You have the opportunity to stand out if you remain alert while continuing to do your work effectively and efficiently. As one manager told us, this is the time to ensure that you are recognized by the "movers and shakers."

Most of your colleagues will be distracted

"Employees were distracted a lot from their current work as they had to spend a lot of time on the things concerning the merger which didn't present any value to them directly. Motivation decreased."

Logistics department project manager, consumer products company

---

DON'T HIDE YOUR TALENTS
UNDER A BUSHEL

The moment you are perceived to be average with your peers in the company or within your industry, you can be replaced. You must demonstrate what makes you different – better – than your colleagues. One director of finance who was involved in a number of mergers in the healthcare sector suggested that you should "find out what the new management team are looking for and prove you're good at it." He went on to say that one should even "engineer success" in this area by finding something valuable to the firm (new sales contract, product development advances, implementation of a more efficient processing system, etc.) that might have happened anyway, but that can be attributed to the power of the newly combined company.

Be the best

"Do your job so well that you are recognized as being at the top of the talent pool."

Director of finance and performance, healthcare industry

It's possible to let others know how good you are without everyone thinking that you are a braggart. The "subtle art of self-promotion," as Marshall Loeb, former editor of *Fortune* and *Money* magazines, said in an article in 2007, is important "to ensure that you get the recognition that you deserve." Gina Hernez-Broome, Cindy McLaughlin, and Stephanie Trovas of the Center for Creative Leadership, a non-profit training organization, stated it differently in a book they wrote in 2007 entitled *Selling Yourself without Selling Out*. They suggested that people should "educate up." By this they mean that employees should make sure that those above them in the organization are aware at all times of the work that they're doing. This is especially important when a company is merging, as those in the executive suites will be distracted with other problems and will tend not to focus as they should on what their staff are doing unless it is something directly related to the merger.

It is therefore necessary to find ways to highlight your achievements. Make sure you keep your boss apprised of your activities at all times even if he or she appears to be too busy to note what you're doing. Don't overdo it or it will slip over from being beneficial to being a negative. But make sure it's done on a regular basis: perhaps a weekly chat, email, or call, depending on which way your boss prefers to communicate. Keep it short and make sure it focuses not on you but on what you're doing for the organization or, even better, what you're doing to make your manager look better to his or her boss and among his or her peers. Keep notes of these conversations or messages, as you will want to make sure you do remember clearly what you have said and when. (This may be especially important should you be at risk of being made redundant, as such notes could be critical evidence if your case ultimately requires outside legal assistance and you need to demonstrate that you kept the company informed about what you had been doing.)

Another way to highlight your achievements is to celebrate success. If your team or department has just made a big sale or completed a large project, a great way to make sure that others know about this is to celebrate it publicly with the team that assisted you. You can be sure that others will hear about this – the corporate grapevine appears in most companies to operate faster than the speed of light! Inviting your boss to the celebration ensures that he or she knows about it as well, even if he or she doesn't actually show up at the event.

Be careful. A 2007 survey conducted by SnagAJob.com, a job site for hourly-paid workers, found that of the 7000 people who responded to a poll they conducted, the "kiss-up" (or, as they put it, "the sycophantic brownnoser who is constantly currying favor with the boss") tied with "slacker" as the most annoying type of person to work with. This is why you might want to publicize your own success in terms of what your team has done and not risk the enmity of your colleagues.

STAY AROUND THE OFFICE. BECOME MORE VISIBLE

You need to be one of the hardest workers or at least perceived to be diligent. This may be easier than it would have been prior to the merger announcement, because, as noted above, many of your colleagues will be working less than before because they are distracted by the deal. You will naturally be distracted too, of course, but you have the advantage of knowing that you really do need to work even harder at this time. You'll know as well exactly what else needs to be done so you won't waste time on unhelpful activities that are unlikely to contribute to your strategy for survival.

Need to stand out

"In a period of change, senior management will look out for people that cope with it well and come out winning. My advice is to stand out from the crowd during these periods and do a really good job, rather than using the excuse of disarray to follow the lemmings off the edge of the cliff."

Bank general manager

Part of the perception of hard work comes from just showing up. Spend more time than previously around the office, and if you don't sit where people can see that you are in the office, make sure you are up and about enough so that they do take notice. One simple way to achieve this is to walk to a colleague's desk or office to ask them a question rather than emailing or calling them. This may even take you to different floors where you normally aren't seen, which gives you further opportunities to network, as discussed in Chapter 9.

Other things to do to improve your presence include: not taking vacation during key periods of decision-making, stopping work from home if you've been doing this and you're able to work in the office, and avoiding unnecessary business trips (external industry conferences, for example, unless you need these for networking or they are crucial at this time for landing new business). Other people will have been doing the opposite of these suggestions, feeling that they deserve a break because of the stresses of the merger. You will stand out because others will see you in the office. Likewise, if you have been considering taking advantage of your company's "family-friendly" policies (such as working four days a week, working part-time or full-time from home, or job sharing), now is clearly not the time to take up this benefit.

Here's another benefit to being around the office and being visible. You may hear more rumors than you would have otherwise about changes being made or potential job opportunities. You certainly won't miss (or be the last to know about) any of the official communications.

YOUR OWN TEAM MAY BE YOUR MOST VALUABLE ASSET

Unless you are running your own one-person company – and in that case, if you get acquired you have total control over the terms anyway! – you will be part of a team. Large or small, your teammates are your most important resource in the company (remembering that your boss is potentially not dependable at the time of a merger, as discussed in Chapter 8).

Risks of forgetting about your team-mates

"When there is a threat – the fear of job security – the effect is to forget about the team spirit and worry about Number 1. It's disastrous for everyone ..."

Finance director, leisure industry

When management are selecting individuals to retain in the company after the merger, it has become more likely in recent years that your colleagues will be asked to provide a formal or informal appraisal of you. They may be questioned by the transition or integration team about your ability to assume a new role or even whether you should keep your current role, if you are in competition with your counterparts in the other firm. Your boss may or may not be on the committee that is deciding your future, so the decision-makers may not be as familiar as they should be with the activities of your group and your specific role and past performance. Following the announcement of the merger or acquisition, it is certainly not uncommon today that everyone in the organization needs to reapply for their jobs. This includes providing references. This was the case, for example, for areas where there was overlap in the 2008 acquisition of ABN AMRO by the Royal Bank of Scotland. Not only are you in competition with your counterparts in the other firm but you are also competing with colleagues from your own company who were doing a different job but who apply to do yours.

You want to make sure that your team-mates will speak highly of you and your abilities. In such situations, some staff make an agreement with others on their team about what each will say about the other if asked, as they probably correctly assume that a consistent story about the team's activities and successes will put them and the group in a better light when it is decision time about who will get which jobs.

Your team is a critical part of your network when you are trying to determine what is really happening. Any team member may be the source of a critical piece of information that isn't communicated by other parts of your network or by your manager. Don't forget as well that receptionists, secretaries, and personal assistants often know the most about what's happening.

From an altruistic perspective, you'll feel better if you do your best for your staff; selfishly, you may also need them in the new organization and therefore you don't want them to leave. One partner in a professional services firm suggested communicating more on a one-to-one level with the team to help put individuals at ease – this intimacy not only helps your intelligence gathering but certainly should contribute to the team operating more effectively post-acquisition, as you have established new ways of communicating more often.

THE POLITICAL GAME

Politics will always play a role, even in firms that claim to be above politics or small companies where the organizational structure is very flat. The politics of any organization will become even more intense during the build-up to a merger or acquisition as everyone is jockeying for the best positions – or even any position! It is best to acknowledge this fact, rather than ignore it.

Spotlight: Strategic Health Authority

Effective use of politics

"The directors in the smaller of two merging Health Trusts played the politics of one merger by first identifying that

> the Chief Executive of the larger trust was not in fact likely to be appointed Chief Executive of the merged trust. They therefore forged links with the Chairman of the larger trust while retaining the confidence of the non-executive directors in the smaller trust. Using links with the Regional Health Authority (as it was called then) to become the preferred Director of Finance to lead the two organizations' finance work stream in the run up to the merger, one executive thereby maneuvered himself into an advantageous position post-merger."
>
> *Director of finance, strategic*
> *health authority, England*

As one executive in a technology company in Eastern Europe told us, he purposely linked himself closely to a CEO who was perceived by most in the firm to be politically skilled both in the industry and within the company. This CEO was an individual who always kept good relations with multiple board members; in addition, he was very loyal and supportive to his subordinates and expected them to be loyal to him, thus increasing his own support base. Almost everyone he knew described him as a good businessman, which is important as politics alone is often necessary but not sufficient by itself to keep someone employed in a company after a merger.

SHINE, SHINE, SHINE

Not everyone will be skilled at self-promotion and politics. Some people just don't have the confidence to self-promote or play the political game: they don't have the personality to speak up on their own behalf. If you are the kind of a person who usually plays down your own accomplishments, you certainly won't be able to change your personality overnight just because your company's in the midst of a merger. If you can't bring yourself to self-promote, then trying to talk up your team's accomplishments should be the tool to point success in your direction. You *are* part of that team, and you should be able to get some benefit from being a team player. Therefore, try your best to increase your department's visibility and success.

One manager in the finance sector told us: "If an individual adds up all their effort in finding a new job – preparing a *CV*, hunting for roles, preparing for and having interviews – and put that effort into their existing job and targeting well-placed sponsors, the rewards would probably be much better." There can be significant positive benefits for employees who are able to position themselves well.

CHAPTER 12

BE A "DOER"

Senior management have many issues to solve when merging two companies. It is a complicated process of people, systems, suppliers, products, brands – virtually every aspect of a company's operations. For most companies, it is an overwhelming process that they get wrong: most deals do ultimately fail.

Stress at the top of the company during a deal

"In a merger situation, senior staff are often under enormous stress and if you are content with your job and feel confident it will be safe, then getting your head down and avoiding the politics is a sensible option."

Finance employee, finance firm

The previous chapter discussed how self-promoting, communicating through your team, and playing the political game can all change senior management's perception of your work and value to the firm. This chapter discusses the critical real work required behind that – as perceptions will go only so far if not based on demonstrated ability and performance.

People are the secret of M&A success. That is, when deals do actually succeed, it is because of the effort of many employees throughout the two companies. They may be helped by outsiders who will include strategy management consultants, human resources advisors, investment bankers, commercial bankers, due diligence investigators, accountants, public relations and communication experts, system integrators, marketing specialists, and many more. The best that these people can do is to provide advice that still needs to be implemented by the people inside the company. Ultimately, it must be the employees of the company who make the deal work.

FIRST IMPRESSIONS

You need to get off the starting blocks quickly. In Chapter 4, there was discussion about how individuals go through phases from denial through anger and eventually to acceptance if not even excitement about the deal. If you are able to move through these steps quickly, you will be at an advantage over those who deal with the announcement of the takeover more slowly. Therefore, try to look ahead at the potential of the deal and not backwards at what is being left behind. Every merger or acquisition has the potential to be a great deal if the management and employees can unite to realize that potential: even some bad deals (those that were made for all the wrong reasons, yet still proceeded to closing) can be turned around.

From the perspective of an individual employee seeking to remain in the company after the merger, it will be important to be seen as one of those who support senior management in their effort to make the deal work, and the sooner the better. Management decisions about who to retain will often be based on how employees react in those first days and weeks following the announcement of the merger.

Only one first impression's possible

"It's very clear that different behaviors will affect the initial perception of the individual. There's only one chance to make a first impression."

Managing director, finance firm

GET INVOLVED EARLY

Keep up to date with as much information as possible on potential M&A deals in your industry, including all of the latest rumors; it's also important to validate rumors if you can as they may not fully or accurately reflect reality. If appropriate, it may even be worth cultivating journalists who often are the first outside a small internal group to be told that a deal is pending.

By keeping on top of the news about M&A deals, you can often anticipate when your own company might be an acquirer or target. For example, if two of your major competitors announce a merger, or if a major competitor acquires a supplier or distributor, your own company's senior management may be considering the same. As shown in Chapter 2, merger and acquisition activity goes in waves, and these always have smaller waves by industry that are sometimes out of synch with the overall market trend. The external business and economic factors that drive your competitor to do a deal are likely to be the same ones that are affecting your company.

If possible, become part of the merger planning and design process. Ideally, you will then get to know about a specific deal before it is announced. Individuals who are members of the planning teams have the greatest knowledge – at least in the beginning – about the rationale behind the deal, the goals and objectives. They even know the other organization best and, if it's a friendly deal, will already have had contact with the other company and, therefore, will be some of the first to know people on the other side.

Value of integration project experience

"I had very interesting responsibilities during integration so I got very valuable experience. I considered this process as an opportunity to get good experience in the short term."

Credit control accountant, consumer products industry

It may not be possible to be on that planning team, and there are downsides to being in that group anyway. Such people are usually part of an internal strategy or corporate development department that continually looks at new possible combinations for the company, as well as divestment opportunities for spinning off parts of the company that are no longer key. These departments are typically – even in very large organizations – very lean: five or six people in total is common, although as a particular large project takes shape they can grow in size by borrowing experts from other parts of the company. Although sometimes these professional planners are later asked to take a management role in an acquisition, typically they act as internal advisors and return to their planning roles to look for the next merger, acquisition, or divestment opportunity. The opportunity for most employees would be at the time when the project needs those additional internal experts as it ramps up in size before a pending deal is announced or immediately thereafter.

Previous experience helpful

"Once you have been through the process a couple of times you know what to expect and you can add value during the process by assisting with integration issues."

Supervisor and team leader, financial services and insurance firm

---

Therefore, try to position yourself – volunteer – to assist with the acquisition effort as an expert from your department. Although this can, as noted above, happen before the deal becomes public, this typically happens once the deal has been announced and the company has said that they need to put together a number of planning and integration teams to bring the two companies together after they have officially merged. These teams can sometimes be formed for a very specific task (for example, choosing which of the two legacy payroll systems will be retained) or can be more general (such as deciding how a sales department should be organized – by product or client – and then determining how the existing salespeople are allocated their work). Some teams will be together for only one meeting, yet others can last for a year or more and thus well beyond the moment when the two companies are officially joined. You therefore need to be prepared to leave your current job in order to work on these merger planning and integration teams.

Focus on integration

"What would I have done differently? I would have given up my regular job to focus entirely on the integration project."

Associate, professional services firm

What are the advantages of being on these teams?

- You get to know best the business of the other company and you will make contact with key individuals from the other side: and just as you are then more likely to land a good position after the deal is over, so will they, and thus they are likely to be an important part of your future network.
- You will be the first to know what is happening with the deal, including personally useful information (which may include whether your own position is one that is likely to be retained in the new organization and where the best opportunities for growth will likely be in the newly combined company if you want to change to a different or more challenging role).
- You will be considered more valuable – as you are one of a small group of people who will know the other company better than most of your colleagues. You presumably will have proven your skills in a high profile position: you can be certain that senior management will have been looking at the integration teams and their output.

Advantages of being on the integration team

"I was a member of the integration team. I was trying to work hard so they could see me in action. But I was working for P&G before I moved to Gillette. So I was surprised when they made an offer as I knew P&G didn't like to take people back."

Country leader of IT marketing, Gillette, then Procter & Gamble

---

All senior and most middle managers will likely be asked to be involved in the merger planning and design process to some degree. They will not be able to avoid being included in the process because it does, with most mergers and acquisitions, affect all departments in some fashion. Many of these senior and middle managers (especially on the business and sales sides of the company) will try to get out of this responsibility or will provide only the minimum that they possibly can to the merger effort. They initially see mergers and acquisitions as a distracting activity from their "day job," especially if they feel secure in their job, or they may only do the absolute minimum for the firm's integration because they are focused on keeping their own job secure. Don't fall into this trap.

In fact, try to become even more involved. For those who are not always given access to the inner sanctums of the company, you may even get to know about the deal before it is announced – which is not always automatically the case for some (the head of human resources, for example, where studies have consistently shown that the HR department is usually consulted very late in the merger planning process (see Chapter 3) and despite the fact that they should be consulted much earlier, if not even being part of the initial planning group).

As a member of the planning team, you will be better able to find out when human resources and management decisions will be made, and by whom. As noted above, this will allow you to position yourself better when revised roles and responsibilities are discussed and you may even be in a position to influence the design of a future role that only you can fill. You will also be able to make connections in the other company to gain support – important even if your firm is the lead in the transaction. In almost every merger, the newly merged entity will include managers from both sides, and while these new managers will typically favor their own staff, as also noted in Chapter 3, they will normally want some representation from the other side in an effort to appear fair to both employee groups.

Show how you'll deliver

"Get involved in the transition activity but only when you can add real value. Use the opportunity to display your skills and competencies. Demonstrate what you would deliver to the future organization."

Chief operating officer, large European bank

Being on the planning team can enable junior staff to shine in front of influential senior managers. As one junior manager in a professional services firm put it: "Look out for the people who will have a say in the new organization – stay very close to them." Or, as expressed more cynically by a senior manager in an IT/ telecoms firm: "Be part of the inner circle who are looking after themselves ... [In our case] they controlled the information to the acquirer to show themselves in a better light."

Promotion is possible, too

"I was part of an organization that was sold to a large US corporate. Office morale was very low leading up to the merger. I avoided getting involved and asked to be part of the integration team. I got to know who the decision-makers were and I was promoted."

Manager, finance firm

In most deals, the first 100 days after the official merger or acquisition marks the intense period of integration when any last major decisions about merging the companies will be made that had not been decided before the deal closing. Even if you haven't been involved before, this period is still an excellent one to be involved with the integration. Beyond then, be careful not to be so vital to the integration team that they ask you to be part of any of the post-100-day post-merger integration teams as well. These may drag on for years in some mergers. Unfortunately, individuals with these teams sometimes find that they cannot then be assigned to a plum job in the new organization when one appears as they are considered too critical to the long-term integration process, and they may even lose their ability to return to their former department once their integration team disbands.

And one last word of advice from one finance director about being on the planning and integration teams: "Don't recommend big cost efficiencies, as you might be one of them!"

PERFORM

Employees are key to the long-term success of the deal because it is they who must be the implementers. The doers. These are the people who are committed to putting in the extra effort to change two ordinary (and maybe even struggling) companies into one better one, while at the same time dealing with a massive reorganization with all the chaos and uncertainty that such a change includes. Remember the survey results shown in Figure 1.1 in Chapter 1: the action most recommended by people who had lived through an M&A deal was to "find ways to add value" and the second action was to "be proactive."

Do your job well

"The biggest mistake is to be unproductive. The best thing to do to survive is not to get distracted. Just do your job. Continue to do what you're doing and don't risk being seen to be someone standing all day by the water cooler and complaining."

Deputy chairman, New York-based bank

It isn't surprising that those who are the most helpful to the two companies while they're in the merger process are often the employees rewarded with the best positions in the new organization post-merger. If you want to stay, you need to be perceived to be a keeper. Rarely will staff who were integral to the design of the deal be fired, assuming that they have done a good job, of course.

Just do the work

"Business people didn't care whether I was from the acquirer or target, they just wanted to see the work."

Head of legal, European bank

These performers are the ones who make themselves indispensable. They identify and understand their unique skills that make them of value to the new organization. Sometimes this will entail some retooling of your skill base or figuring out how to apply your existing skills in a different way. If time and money allow, consider a training course to fill in a gap in your skill set.

Be committed

"The key to survival in my experience of two different mergers is to make yourself invaluable by demonstrating your corporate knowledge and at the same time your willingness to embrace the changes, 'going the extra mile' in terms of commitment to delivering the changes."

Director of finance, accounting firm

As a director of finance and performance in the healthcare industry told us, "Make sure you don't stop doing your job well because you fear or expect redundancies in the merged organization." Another executive advised us to "ensure now that information requests are dealt with promptly and to be flexible" and went on to tell us the following story.

"Can do" attitude

"Following the merger, my post was changed and my old job was undertaken by someone from the other organization. I adopted a 'can do' attitude and continued to assist even though it was no longer my job. After eight months, the jobs were merged and following a competition, I was appointed to the single post."

Deputy director of finance, hospital

"BE A TEACHER"

Part of what you do is both how you do it and what you know about your job and the rest of the organization. As one interviewee said, especially if you work for the target company, you need to show that you're valued for what is in your head.

When a company is acquired, the new owners should have done a lot of due diligence on the target, trying to make sure that they clearly know what they are purchasing, including ensuring that they understand how best to integrate the two companies once the deal is completed. Most experienced deal-makers also know that no matter how extensive their due diligence, there remains a lot that they don't know, either because they didn't have enough time or resources to look into the target as much as they would have liked, or perhaps they didn't know which questions to ask. The chairman of the board of Deutsche Bank, following its acquisition of Bankers Trust in 1999 when several problems in the target became apparent only after the deal closed despite a very intensive due diligence process, commented: "You have to get much closer before they tell you such things." Although his comment was in specific response to the unpopularity of the chairman and CEO of Bankers Trust, he could have been referring to positive aspects of the company as well.

Therefore, if you are an expert in an area – and anyone in the target at the start of the deal is more of an expert at knowing the target than anyone in the acquirer – you may have the opportunity to share your knowledge of the company with key people from the buyer once the deal is a certainty. Some suggested that you should not be shy about this. You have to find ways to make contact with the buyer's decision-makers and assist by giving them the knowledge that they need to make the deal successful.

What you know

"Be a teacher. Most of the time the executives of the newly-acquired organization will know less about your business than they will let on. Offering to explain historical perspectives, customer nuances, and where the company has had prior success and failure will be greatly valued. The time right after a deal is when you want to be valued for 'What you Know,' not necessarily for 'What you Do'."

Rich Aiello, Welsh, Carson, Anderson & Stowe,
private equity investment firm

KEEP YOUR CLIENTS AND KEEP THEM HAPPY

One way to keep your job – whether you work with the integration teams or not – is to have clients who are loyal to you personally. Encourage them to say they give business to the company because of you. The company will be less willing to make you redundant for fear of losing the client – and its revenue. Remember the example in Chapter 5 of Banco Santander's acquisition of Abbey National: Santander announced that no sales staff would be made redundant and that any back office staff who had once worked in the front office could return to sales and be assured of being retained. This case clearly demonstrates the value which executives place on retaining those with revenue responsibility.

Not everyone in the back office has front office experience, and not all acquirers will act as Santander did. When faced with a merger or acquisition, those in back office or middle office positions should think of the front office as their client. Being more at risk of redundancy after a merger, they should also try to link themselves with client-facing teams; at least get those you support internally to speak up positively on your behalf. If the front office team is telling the integration managers that you are key to their revenue-generating ability, you are less likely to be made redundant for fear that the revenues would be at risk without you.

You may even be responsible for making the decision about which of the two companies' legacy systems (payroll, accounts payable, CRM (client relationship management), trading, operations, and other systems) will be retained. Usually, there is a transition period where both companies' systems are maintained until one is phased out in favor of the other. In most cases, the retained system is the acquirer's, but this is not always the case – especially if the target's back office systems are superior and one of the stated reasons that the company was bought. If your job does depend on the continued use of just one of the systems, you may want to ask your "clients" (the front office staff) to push for your system to be retained. Their influence may be greater than yours and could just be the edge needed to put your system on top.

System selection driving jobs

"When Deutsche Bank acquired BT [Bankers Trust] in 1999, I was in the technology support group for the sales team. There was a similar system in BT supported by their tech support team. The decision was made during the integration to retain the Deutsche Bank head of sales and he said that all transactions would use the Deutsche Bank system. I was safe. But if they'd chosen the BT system, I would have been toast."

Technology support team vice-president, Deutsche Bank

It can be a vicious and unpleasant time. Beware of how internal relationships may change: "Watch out for colleagues who immediately turn into animals, trying to protect and enhance their position in the eyes of the new owners," advised a manager in the media/entertainment sector. Some of the people interviewed for this book felt that during the merger there were even fellow employees who sabotaged the work of others in order to make themselves look better.

Others will change

"Certain people seem to have changed their personalities overnight for the worse."

Legal employee, healthcare and social work organization

BE PATIENT

Although the merger process can be fast paced at times with an intensity of effort not seen before in the company, there are also periods when it seems that nothing is happening and no news is forthcoming. Sometimes these periods are planned by senior management: for example, if the firm has an annual earnings report pending soon, they may have a blackout on any contact with potential merger partners so that, if asked, they can honestly say that they are not currently in contact with any other companies about an acquisition or merger. In other cases, there may simply be no news.

Patience is a virtue

"Prepare to be patient. If you can't be patient, it is better to leave immediately."

Information technology analyst, consumer products industry

It is therefore important to be patient. When the first rumors or even an official announcement of an acquisition appear, many people panic and take irreversible steps such as quickly departing to a competitor or making public statements about what they will do if such a merger occurs. Once the details are revealed, they may regret their decision to act rashly, but it may be too late to recover or return. Similarly, many deals turn out to be very different than originally planned, and making an irreversible decision based on early information – even if from official sources – can be dangerous. As noted earlier, it pays to be flexible at this time.

Best to plan carefully, using many of the suggestions contained in this book and supplemented with any intelligence you uncover about the deal itself and your own knowledge of your company and its managers. Try not to take steps that cannot be changed. Prepare, but don't commit too early. Of course, sometimes the opposite will be true as one banker suggested below.

Decide quickly

"Within the first few weeks make a decision whether you should stay or leave the new organization and then live every day with that goal in mind. Do not use the 'wait and see' tactic because your initial observations and experiences are unlikely to change with time but your frustration will build as individual experiences sway you one way then the other regarding the future."

Chief operating officer, large European bank

THE PAYOFF

Knowledge truly is power during an M&A deal. A secure position adds to that power. If you do think your company will be acquired or be an acquirer, it helps to be of special value to the company. (Of course, this is true at all times, but is especially true during a merger when large numbers of people will be fired and therefore statistically you are more at risk.) Of special value will be active involvement in the merger integration effort. Try actively to be recognized as a "doer" and as someone key to the company's future success.

POSTSCRIPT: *CARPE DIEM*

The M&A market goes up and down. Each new merger wave – the last one peaked in 2007 – sets new records. Even with vast changes in the economy and during recessions, it's a market which continues to power ahead. New entrants emerge who want to buy companies: in the 1980s, it was the leverage buyout funds, the 1990s saw more deals that crossed borders internationally and the rise of technology companies doing large deals with overpriced shares, and early in the new millennium it was the hedge funds, private equity firms, and venture capital companies that added volume to an already strong merger wave.

When the economy slumps, the cost of buying companies declines, bringing further buyers to the market. In 2008 and 2009, governments in the USA, UK, and other major countries were bailing out bankrupt or almost-bankrupt companies, principally in the banking sector but also in the automobile, housing and con-struction, transportation, and other industries. Sovereign wealth funds from the Middle East and Asia continue to have an appetite for purchasing large stakes in companies and targeting major industries.

This will likely continue, as when one player steps off the stage, it seems that there's always another ready to come on. The curtain hasn't closed on the M&A deal market. You can be certain that there will continue to be many more deals in the future. After several record years for mergers and acquisitions, most experts are predicting that the decline in merger activity that started in the second half of 2007 will continue for at least a couple of years. Yet most experts will also agree that the long-term trend – despite these temporary setbacks – is for more and more merger activity.

Looking towards the future of M&A, two things will never change: first, a large number will fail to deliver what the architects of the deals promised and second, whether the deal is successful or not, people will lose their jobs when companies combine.

Value in surviving an M&A deal

"There's only one way to deal with a take-over. Realize from day one that you are now working in the corporate equivalent of a construction zone. Things will fall on you without warning. So, you can either be a victim and get hurt by flying debris, or you can get yourself a hard hat. By the time this thing is all over, you'll have gained a tremendous amount of experience – not the least in leading in a time of chaos. That will make you not just a better leader, but a very valuable one, too."

Rudi Plettinx, Managing Director of the European Operations of the Center for Creative Leadership, Brussels, Belgium, as quoted in the blog, The Exec-Ed Zone

---

Many people get fired, but many people survive as well. It's also an unfortunate fact that some of the survivors are not the best qualified or most experienced from the wide choice of internal candidates in the pre-merger companies. Politics and luck play roles in who survives, or maybe even an outsider is brought in. Some people are demoted to a more junior role.

Better lucky

"I was lucky. My boss was selected to stay with the firm. The guy who did his job at the other company was fired because they didn't need both of them. It could have gone either way, as both had great reputations.

"Of course, my boss wanted to surround himself mainly with people he knew well and trusted, so most of us stayed from his team. I guess you could say I was lucky it was my boss who was kept, because certainly the people from the other company could have done just as well in my job as I do."

Vice-president, technology, European bank

You don't need to leave it all up to chance. This book has discussed some "tricks of the trade" suggested to us by many who survived. They told us and demonstrated that you are able to improve your chances of being a survivor if your company's acquired. There are, of course, no guarantees that a job can be retained or found in the newly combined company, but an application of the recommendations discussed in the preceding chapters should improve the odds immensely.

Every deal's different

"Even after 40 deals, each one brings new challenges and new situations which have not been experienced before, whether during the deal itself or in post-acquisition integration."

Senior executive, utilities firm

You may feel secure. Your company is doing well, and you are, too. But the best-run companies are often the most attractive acquisition or merger candidates *because* they are successful. It is difficult in today's business environment to have a full career where you will not at some point experience a merger or an acquisition. Many employees live through multiple deals.

When companies merge, job losses typically range from as few as one in 10 up to one in every seven employees, but sometimes in rare cases even as high as one in three. What does this mean? Look around in the office. Look at the person on your left and on your right. In an acquisition where redundancies are high, one of you will be made redundant; if you are in a particularly unlucky department, it may be the entire team. Approximately 18 000 people were made redundant in the HP/Compaq "merger" in just two years; projected redundancies because of the purchase of Dutch Bank ABN AMRO in 2007 were reported to be 19 000 but then ended up much higher (perhaps also as a result of the banking crisis), and in another banking deal, Thomson Reuters reported that 24 000 employees would be made redundant after Bank of America has finished its acquisition of Merrill Lynch. The risk is virtually always that you will lose your job because mergers that create jobs, at least in the short term, are virtually non-existent. It certainly is useful to know about survival techniques that have proven helpful to others when faced with a possible, pending, or ongoing merger or acquisition.

As discussed in earlier chapters, the attrition rate is rarely spread evenly across the newly combined workforce. The higher up you are in the organization, the more likely that your position has a comparable incumbent on the other side. It is not uncommon to have as many as three-quarters of senior managers in the acquired company leaving within three years. The more senior you are in the firm, the higher the chance you will be made redundant in a merger. After all, as we have discussed, what company needs two heads of marketing or two finance directors? And co-CEOs (or co-positions at any level) rarely last long. At those levels, your chances of survival are 50/50 at best, as maybe even both will be fired and a new senior executive team brought in.

Risk of redundancy at senior levels

"In the end, only one member of the top management team of the acquired company was still with the merged company after two years – and that was in an area where the acquiring company had a clear senior personnel void in a key position."

Partner, US real estate development company

Strangely, then, the trip to the top of the business world is often determined by an individual's success in surviving by effective maneuvering upwards through a number of mergers and acquisitions. Once near the top, senior executives may even design a merger in order to improve their own personal power where they believe their success is assured. Even if the deal isn't manipulated in any selfish way by a CEO or board member (although it is difficult to imagine a deal where the CEO's hubris doesn't play some role), in modern business many do feel that the easiest way to progress to a senior management position is through promotions achieved during mergers or acquisitions.

It is not just your level in the organization that increases your chances of being made involuntarily redundant. As noted earlier, if the acquisition is hostile and you are in the target company, you are more likely to lose your job than if the deal was friendly. Headquarters and support areas (IT especially, but also including finance and human resources) are usually disproportionately at risk. Geography can be a factor too: those working in the relatively flexible employment markets of the USA and UK may be more at risk than employees in continental Europe, where staff reductions tend to take place more through attrition. Some, however, are just lucky. But there are others who know how to play the acquisition survival game best.

Throughout the book, I have been discussing the actions that you can take if you want to improve the odds of being retained rather than fired when your company has decided to merge, be acquired, or to acquire another company. The flip side of those actions is often clear: if you should be a "doer," for example when you want to retain your job, then being the opposite (a "slacker") is obviously to be avoided. General good business practice is still necessary: as suggested earlier, you should be perceived as someone who has a positive attitude about the company and about the specific merger or acquisition under way; this means, of course, that you should not openly criticize the merger process and how management are handling the deal.

One of the biggest myths during a merger is that those with merit will be recognized and retained. Employees falsely assume that if they are better than their peers, this will be noted and they therefore are not at risk of being demoted or made redundant. Nothing could be further from the truth. In fact, leaving your corporate future totally to chance may be the most dangerous decision. If you do rely on luck, you run the risk that you will be fired. The secret of surviving a merger is instead to have a plan which seeks to protect your position and may even identify ways to exploit the situation and be promoted.

Just as individuals may be differently exposed according to seniority, job type, whether they work for the target or acquirer, and whether the deal is hostile, so survival strategies should be personalized. For some, a merger will be a great excuse to leave: such individuals should therefore plan an exit strategy to secure a job from another firm. In similar situations, many employees have been able to start work in new positions while simultaneously taking advantage of what are often relatively generous redundancy terms and thus "double dip."

The need to continue to be vigilant about your job doesn't end with the first announcement of redundancies or the appointment of the team during the merger transition. Remember the research quoted in Chapter 1 that showed that executive turnover is higher for *nine* years in firms that merged than those that haven't. You need to continue to perform at a level that is going to make you recognized.

DEVELOP A PLAN

Career coaching, continual job improvement, "pushing the envelope," "thinking outside the box," and all the other business phrases quoted in the self-help section of your local book store will certainly come in handy, although only you know what will work best for you and in your new organization.

This translates into a need for a thoughtful plan, utilizing all of the ideas and suggestions that have been provided in this book. As noted in the first chapter, all of the tips for survival must be read within the context of what will work within your specific company for the current deal and what is appropriate to your own situation and personality. Talking with your network and making an honest assessment of what can really work, you will know best what that plan should be. Actions taken in the first few days following an announcement will need to be adjusted as further information becomes available. Some strategies will work, others not. You will need to be willing to change and adapt your plan for survival, looking at what is working for others in the company as well.

Any plan needs to be based on good information – whether for preparing for the worst or using the deal to get ahead. Unfortunately, in the uncertainty surrounding an M&A transaction, accessing accurate information, although vital, will be difficult, as discussed. This doesn't mean that you should panic and make hasty career decisions. "Ensure you have all the available information before making any decisions about your future," recommends one banker. Several senior managers have told us that they got the position which they wanted because they were willing to wait for others to leave.

In developing your plan for survival, keep in mind as well some of the following behaviors that have been found to be helpful when dealing with change:

- Don't think your future will be determined by one big decision (either the company's or yours); plan for many small steps, see how they work, and then be willing to change strategy and tactics if necessary.
- Consider your survival in your job as a job itself; be dedicated to it and spend all the time necessary to make sure you succeed. Do not be distracted.
- Devote your time and energy to managing situations over which you have some control or influence. From a personal stress management perspective, if you have no control over a situation, it can be both stressful and frustrating to spend a lot of effort trying to change something you can't. Plus, it doesn't get you anywhere.
- Step back occasionally and try to see your plan and progress through the eyes of others in the firm; this pause also gives time for reflection and a chance to recharge your batteries.
- Develop alternatives: at some point it may just become necessary to leave or to change your plan dramatically. Don't put all your eggs in one basket.

This book has covered behavioral actions that you can take (such as being proactive and performing), altering perceptions about the deal both of yourself and others around you (making sure that you keep a positive attitude and even volunteer to serve on a transition team), impression management (especially by carefully promoting your capabilities to the decision-makers in the company), time management (through being patient, yet also by acting quickly after the deal announcement), and communication and information processing (by asking questions and getting as much information as you can about the deal and its aftermath). Complex as it may appear, these all can be combined into an effective plan to survive the merger or acquisition. The quotes and Spotlights throughout the book show that real people have done it, and have done it well – and in the process emerged with additional skills that can help them not just to survive the next deal, but in business generally.

Surviving the deal helped develop core skills

"Each M&A situation I have been involved in has developed relevant skills, i.e. adaptability, change management, and the ability to look at situations objectively."

Head of HR, financial services and insurance firm

Ideally, you will find a way to exploit rather than just survive the M&A process, and your plan should anticipate this possibility as well. And whether someone thrives rather than simply survives may also be linked to their role within an organization and the nature of transaction. For example, in our surveys, we found that those more likely to exploit the M&A situation to enhance their career came predominantly from the target firm. For them, the transaction appeared to provide a catalyst for changing existing structures and practices, and offered the opportunity to free themselves from constraints within their prior organizations, including leaving and getting another better job. Being from the target, they felt more at risk and thus were willing to be more proactive in trying quickly to secure their future. The same survival tips that helped those in a target company could have been used by the acquirer's employees, too.

Do not sit tight, doing nothing and expecting that you will survive. Even if you think that you are secure, taking the steps discussed in this book will improve your chances of survival. You must act. *Carpe diem.* And good luck.

KEY TERMS IN MERGERS AND ACQUISITIONS

Acquisition

When one company (the "buyer") purchases a second, usually smaller, company (the "target"); the second company ceases to exist and the assets of the target are then controlled by the buyer. The employees of the target now work for the buyer (excepting those employees fired as part of the acquisition process). If both companies cease to exist and a third company is created from the two legacy companies, the term generally used to describe the deal is "merger."

Analyst

Also sometimes called "researcher," this is the entry-level client-facing position in most investment banking M&A departments. Analysts usually are hired directly from university and join after receiving their undergraduate degree. Most stay with the bank for two years (sometimes three) before either returning to university for their MBA or are (more rarely) promoted (see "associate"). The term "analyst" also refers to the individuals in a bank or other equity research institution who provide market research on companies.

Announcement date

The formal and public disclosure of a pending M&A deal. Prior to announcement, there may be rumors in the market about the deal and even leaks, but they have not been confirmed. The announcement is usually made through a press release and perhaps a press conference at which the CEO of the purchaser and often the target are available for questioning by journalists and market analysts. If the company is listed on a stock exchange, the exchange will also need to be informed on announcement day and, depending on the deal, other regulators may also need to be informed.

Associate

This is the position in most investment banking M&A departments where employees begin to have responsibility for the creation of analyses and reports for clients. They will be supported by and supervise analysts on specific projects and train those analysts in analytical skills. Most associates have no staff reporting to them full-time (except on a project basis). In some firms, there is a further intermediate step in the promotion ladder of "senior associate," which is also sometimes called "assistant vice-president."

Auction

When two or more companies are competing to buy the target. This usually results in a higher price for the target but increases the time when there is uncertainty on the part of employees of the target as to their eventual owner.

Bear hug

When the bidder makes a very high offer for the target in an attempt to gain quick acceptance by the target's management and board, and to prevent other bidders from taking over the target. Most bear hug offers include the implicit threat that the bidder will make a hostile takeover offer if the target board does not accept the bear hug offer.

Bulge bracket investment bank

Within the M&A industry, this refers to an elite group of global investment banking advisory firms who will typically do the most number and value of deals year after year.

The City

A term to denote the area in London where banks traditionally were located. Geographically, it comprises the area (approximately a square mile in size, and thus also sometimes called "The Square Mile") that was contained within London's Roman walls.

Closing

The day during the merger or acquisition process when the two companies formally become one: if an acquisition, it will be the day when the target company ceases to exist and is absorbed into the buyer; for a merger, it is when both companies cease to operate and a new company is formed from those two companies.

Conglomerate

A company that is composed of divisions that are generally unrelated to each other and where few synergies can be gained through the combination of those businesses. A conglomerate acquisition is one where the buyer's existing group of businesses is unrelated to any of the businesses of the target.

Divestiture (or "spin-off")

The sale of a business, usually an entire division or a product line. This is sometimes planned when a company makes an acquisition because (1) for regulatory (monopoly or competition) reasons the buyer would otherwise have too large a business or (2) the buyer purchased the target for specific assets and never intended to keep some unrelated assets of the target and therefore is now unloading them.

Due diligence

The process during an M&A deal whereby one company investigates the details, often looking at non-public information, of the other company. Due diligence can be conducted without actually contacting the other company, but normally refers to the process when access to the target company is granted to a purchaser (or among the two companies in a merger).

First 100 days

The period immediately after closing when the two companies begin their integration. This "first 100 days" is normally a time of intense activity when key decisions about the newly combined companies are implemented and also when most of the employees who are going to be made redundant will be informed. Integration continues after this time, but at a lower level of activity in most areas.

Friendly acquisition

From the target company's perspective, this is a deal that is agreed by management. The target company's management will recommend that the company's shareholders approve the deal. In a friendly deal, the target usually agrees to let the buyer have access to confidential information before closing.

Golden parachute/silver parachute/tin parachute

Special compensation arrangements (special bonus, stock options, vesting of previously awarded compensation) between a company and its senior executives in case the company is acquired. Sometimes any acquisition will trigger the golden parachute, but in other cases it is triggered only when the deal is hostile. Usually, the golden parachute award will be significant in comparison to the executive's normal compensation. "Silver parachutes" refer to similar awards granted to lower level executives and even senior managers; "tin parachutes" are similar awards granted to all employees below those levels.

Hedge fund

Hedge funds are investment vehicles for high net worth individuals who invest in a variety of different classes of investments, including (as related to M&A deals) the shares of publicly listed companies and privately held companies. Each fund will have a particular investment strategy but these can vary greatly between funds. They traditionally have had minimal regulation from government authorities but may be more tightly regulated in the future.

Hostile takeover

From the target company's perspective, this is an unwelcome attempt by a buyer to purchase the company. In most hostile takeovers, the target company's senior executives and board of directors will actively resist the purchase through actions taken to defeat the purchaser (including finding a friendlier buyer) and will recommend to its shareholders that they vote against the purchase if the deal proceeds that far. If a deal is not hostile, it will be called a "friendly takeover."

Investment bank

Usually, the principal advisor on an M&A deal. The investment banker will have many responsibilities during the deal, but most often will coordinate the activities of other advisors, identify potential target companies (or buyers, if representing a company for sale), provide advice on structuring the deal and the pricing (including arranging financing if required), and generally support senior management of the target or buyer during the deal. Some investment banks can provide the financing as well, whereas other specialist investment banks may provide only the advisory work.

Leverage

Commonly used to indicate a company or deal that has or uses a large amount of debt, typically at a level over one-third of the total financing.

Magic Circle law firm

The elite group of leading global law firms based in London.

Merger

When two companies agree to combine all their operations to create a third company, while at the same time exchanging all of the assets and ownership of the two legacy companies for the new third company. The two legacy companies therefore cease to exist. In most mergers, the two legacy companies are usually of similar size, or else it is more likely that the deal will be structured as an "acquisition." Most mergers are friendly. Note that common usage applies the term "merger" to many transactions that should strictly be called "acquisitions."

Outplacement

Firms or individual consultants who provide advice and support to employees who have been or will be made redundant. Most outplacement firms are paid by the company that has made the employee redundant, but individuals can also pay for these services themselves if their firms do not.

Post-merger integration

The period that starts upon the closing of a deal but that can last anywhere from a few months to a number of years. The post-merger integration is the time in an acquisition when all of the operations of the target company are absorbed into the buyer; if the deal was structured as a merger, then this is the time when the operations of both legacy companies are combined.

Private equity firm

An investment manager who will purchase the equity of companies that are not publicly listed on a stock exchange (and therefore privately traded). Private equity firms, as with venture capital firms and hedge funds, will usually plan to sell their equity at a later point after having made a certain profit on the shares that they own. See also "Venture capital firm."

Synergy

This is the 1 + 1 = 3 effect where the impact of two companies combining creates a stronger company than the sum of the two companies when they were independent of each other. Expense synergies (including headcount reductions) refer to the situation following a merger or acquisition where functions that were duplicated across the two companies can now be reduced when they are combined (e.g. there's only need for one CEO, not two).

Takeover

Usually, a term denoting an unfriendly (see "Hostile takeover") bid for a company, but can refer to any merger or acquisition.

Venture capital firm

A venture capital firm is an investment manager who will purchase the equity of start-up or relatively new, early-stage growth companies before they are publicly listed on a stock exchange. This investment in the company's equity will allow it to fund its next stage of growth. See also "Private equity firm."

Wall Street

The location in New York City of the New York Stock Exchange and, in the streets surrounding Wall Street, the original headquarters of many of the largest banks and investment banks in the USA.

White Knight

A friendly acquirer sought by the target to purchase the company instead of a hostile bidder.

ACKNOWLEDGEMENTS

I am certainly indebted to many people for the help they have provided in putting this book together. There have been hundreds of individuals who have told me how they survived a merger or acquisition, and many who didn't survive but wanted to share their stories as well.

A number of students at Cass Business School in London have assisted with this work over the past several years, putting in numerous hours conducting interviews and researching the topic. Special thanks need to go to Svetlana Bolshakova, Garth Leonard, Anita Longman, Andrew Little, Maria Nakhodkina, Girish Ramadurgam, Omiros Sarikas and Gulmira Zhanarystanova. Other students in my classes – too numerous to mention – have also provided advice and assistance. Many of these students from my executive courses have shared with me their tips and suggestions for how they avoided redundancy when their employers combined in an M&A deal; they also provided observations about things that they wished they had not done or that they had observed others doing which should be avoided.

Two surveys used in this book should be noted specifically. In the largest of these surveys, conducted by graduate students Mark Dickenson and Gareth Wood, over 800 questionnaires were distributed and 166 people responded, an estimated response rate of 20%. One hundred and twenty-two completed the entire survey. Of those, approximately one-third were C-level executives (CEO, CFO, COO, or managing director), 18% head of function, 21% in other management positions, 10% supervisors, and the remainder employees without management responsibility. Seventy percent had been with their company at least two years prior to their latest M&A deal. Fifty-two percent were in targets and 48% in acquirers. The sample had a disproportionate number of male respondents (80%) due most likely to the fact that 50% of the respondents were in the finance industry but other industries represented included (in order of respondents) telecommunications, professional services, manufacturing, legal, health care, leisure industries, education, government, hospitality, information technology, marketing and public relations, non-profit organizations, real estate, retail, travel, utilities, and wholesale. The results of this survey also provided the information for the "Top Tips" shown in this book. Thank you, Mark and Gareth.

Another series of interviews was conducted by students Amy Howlett and Simon Solomon. All of the 23 people invited to participate from a cross-section of the investment banking and legal sectors worked primarily or exclusively in the M&A sector within their firms. Sixteen interviews were conducted. No measurable differences could be identified between those who participated and those who did not. The 16 were asked 31 set questions that covered topics related to the individual's background, working environment, motivations, career progression, anecdotes and illustrative stories, and skills. Some interviewees drew on experience from several firms. Thanks, Amy and Simon, for conducting these lengthy interviews (and thanks to those who offered their time to speak with them confidentially).

My background is in investment banking and consulting, having worked for almost 25 years at Morgan Stanley, Booz Allen & Hamilton (now Booz & Co.), and Deutsche Bank, and thus I would like to thank many of my former colleagues who have helped me understand better the business of M&A and who remain as friends and business associates. I asked many for their advice about this book. Particular thanks to David Hartman, John Kurtz, Nick McDonagh, Dr. Sybille Hofmann, David Mellor, Thure Meyer, and George Schaefer. Likewise, after leaving the investment banking world, I became an executive coach and had, over the course of a number of years, over 100 clients from large, global organizations, many of whom were facing redundancy (or had been made redundant) due to mergers or acquisitions. Their stories are also used in this book, with permission, of course.

From former colleagues, classmates, students, clients, and structured interviews, I have included many direct quotations throughout the book. In many cases, anonymity was requested. Hopefully, most will recognize their quotations and I hope that I have captured their comments accurately. I am very proud and grateful that you have agreed to be part of this book. Thanks here to Tom Bayne, Keith Bullen, Ray Catindig, Ory Eshel, Steve Robson, George Sidjimkov, Alexandra Stubbings and the many who did request anonymity.

Several faculty members at Cass Business School in London and elsewhere have provided suggestions for this book and in some cases have read sections and given me great advice on how to avoid some errors and make it better. Any errors that still remain are mine. But I do need to thank especially Joanna Zaleska and the expert research assistants at the M&A Research Centre: Eliza Brewka, David Cuming, and Anna Faelten.

Catherine Stokes deserves a special thank you. She has read numerous drafts and proofread versions of this book that, fortunately, will never see the light of day again. Likewise to Ellen Hallsworth and Michaela Fay at John Wiley for their excellent comments on improving this book.

And lastly, my family – although of course they really should be mentioned first. My wife, Daniela, has been very understanding in humoring and supporting me through the mornings, afternoons, evenings, and even nights when I was sitting in front of my computer, talking on the telephone, or away from the house, working to complete this book. Thank you!

OTHER USEFUL READING

Balogun, J. and Hope-Hailey, V. (2004) *Exploring Strategic Change* (2nd edition) (Prentice Hall)

Bragg, S. (2009) *Mergers & Acquisitions: A Condensed Practitioner's Guide* (John Wiley & Sons)

Buono, A.F. and Bowditch, J.L. (1989) *The Human Side of Mergers and Acquisitions: Managing Collisions Between People, Cultures, and Organizations* (Jossey-Bass)

Carey, D. (2000) A CEO roundtable on making mergers succeed. *Harvard Business Review* (May)

Cartwright, S. and Cooper, C.L. (1992) *Mergers and Acquisitions: the Human Factor* (Billing & Sons)

Cartwright, S. and Cooper, G. (1996) *Managing Mergers Acquisitions & Strategic Alliances: Integrating People and Cultures* (Butterworth-Heinemann)

Connor-Smith, J.K. and Flaschbart, C. (2007) Relations between personality and coping: a meta-analysis. *Journal of Personality and Social Psychology*, Vol. 93, No. 6

Doherty, N. and Tyson, S. (1993) *Executive Redundancy and Outplacement* (Saxon Printing)

Galpin, T. and Herndon, M. (2007) *The Complete Guide to Mergers & Acquisitions* (2nd edition) (Jossey-Bass)

Harding, D. and Rouse, T. (2007) Human due diligence. *Harvard Business Review* (April)

Haspeslagh, P.C. and Jemison, D.B. (1991) *Managing Acquisitions: Creating Value Through Corporate Renewal* (The Free Press)

Hernez-Broome, G., McLaughlin, C. and Trovas, S. (2007) *Selling Yourself Without Selling Out* (CCL Press)

Hewlett, S.A. and Buck Luce, C. (2006) Extreme jobs: the dangerous allure of the 70-hour workweek. *Harvard Business Review* (December)

Ibarra, H. (2004) *Working Identity* (Harvard Business School Press)

Jolles, R. (2005) *The Way of the Road Warrior* (Jossey Bass)

Kay, I. and Shelton, M. (2000) The people problem in mergers. *McKinsey Quarterly*, 4

Kotter, J.P. (1982) *The General Managers* (Free Press)

McManus, M.L. and Hergert, M.L. (1988) *Surviving Merger & Acquisition* (Scott, Foresman and Company)

Mintzberg, H. (1973) *The Nature of Managerial Work* (Harper & Row)

Mirvis, P.H. and Marks, M.L. (1992) *Managing the Merger* (Prentice Hall)

Moeller, S. and Brady, C. (2007) *Intelligent M&A: Navigating the Mergers and Acquisitions Minefield* (John Wiley & Sons)

Naficy, M. (1997) *The Fast Track: The Insider's Guide to Winning Jobs in Management Consulting, Investment Banking and Securities Trading* (Broadway Books)

Pilbeam, S. and Corbridge, M. (2002) *People Resourcing: HRM in Practice* (2nd edition) (Pearson Education)

Rousseau, D. (1996) *Psychological Contracts in Organizations: Understanding Written and Unwritten Agreements* (Sage)

Sabine, M. (1993) *Corporate Finance: Flotations, Equity Issues and Acquisitions* (2nd edition) (Butterworths)

Sonnenfeld, J. and Ward, A. (2007) *Firing Back: How Great Leaders Rebound After Career Disasters* (Harvard Business School Press)

Sudarsanam, S. (2003) *Creating Value from Mergers and Acquisitions: The Challenges* (FT Prentice Hall/Pearson Education)

Westergaard, J., Noble, I. and Walker, A. (1989) *After Redundancy: The Experience of Economic Insecurity* (Polity Press)

INDEX

Compiled by Indexing Specialists (UK) Ltd